FRANÇOISE HENRY IN CO. MAYO
The Inishkea Journals

08.07.2014.

For Fr Tom Cawley,

To remind you of

your Roots.

+ John Fleming

Françoise Henry in Co. Mayo
The Inishkea Journals

Janet T. Marquardt
EDITOR

Huw Duffy
TRANSLATOR

FOUR COURTS PRESS

Typeset in 10.5 pt on 12.5 pt Ehrhardt by
Carrigboy Typesetting Services for
FOUR COURTS PRESS LTD
7 Malpas Street, Dublin 8, Ireland
www.fourcourtspress.ie
and in North America for
FOUR COURTS PRESS
c/o ISBS, 920 NE 58th Avenue, Suite 300, Portland, OR 97213.

A catalogue record for this title is available
from the British Library.

ISBN 978–1–84682–324–4 hbk
ISBN 978–1–84682–374–9 pbk

SPECIAL ACKNOWLEDGMENT

This publication has received support from the Heritage Council under
the Heritage Education, Community and Outreach Scheme 2012.

Printed in England
by Antony Rowe, Chippenham, Wilts.

For Alice, who shared some of the discoveries

Contents

Acknowledgments

Many people living on the Mullet Peninsula were extraordinarily helpful towards understanding the references to life in that region during the time that Françoise Henry visited: at the Aughleam Heritage Centre, Ionad Deirbhle – Mary Rowan (Maura Gaughan Ruane), Laoise Ní Dhúda and Rosemarie Geraghty. Other people who were willing to be interviewed for their memories or to provide contacts for our research were Pap and Kate Murphy, Margaret Padden Keane with her daughter Kathleen Keane Geraghty, Micky Lavelle, P.J. McGinty, Tom Phete Keane, John Lavelle, Christy O'Reilly, the Quigleys at Léim Siar, Margo Cawley and Mary Bhán Lavelle. In the wider region, we were also helped by Noel O'Neill in Castlebar, and Tom Reilly (Tomás Bán Ó Raghallaigh) and Kathleen Cawley in Ballina.

Making it possible to get to Inishkea North, Sean Lavelle of Lavelle Boat Charters, who was willing to make the trip in rough weather if needed, but with a careful watch on the forecast, took me on the loveliest of days. Sean's understanding of the local topography, the usage of the boats and currachs, and kindness in sharing his knowledge of Inishkea North was invaluable.

Reading suggestions and advice were also given by the artist, Hughie O'Donoghue, who has produced a series of paintings on the theme of the Inishkeas, and by Brian Dornan, whose book on the islands is cited below and who generously helped draw up a map, with Greg Fennell, based upon his profound knowledge of the area. Brilliant polishing of the map was undertaken by Bill Doran. Assistance with flower identifications was provided by Daniel Kelly, John Parnell and Pierre Hiernaux, and with the semaphore tower at Glosh, Joe Dillon. Seamus Caulfield advised on possible sources for the word 'Drak'. For help on the difficult, often phonetic, Irish text, we are grateful to Cathal Ó hÁinle and Ciarán Ó Coigligh. A final, nuanced, reading of the translation was kindly undertaken by Roger Little (in some consultation with Patricia Little), whose mastery of the language provided lessons to us all.

For material on Françoise Henry, we are indebted to the conversations, letters, recommendations and publications of Hilary Richardson, Eileen Kane, Cecil Curle, John and Win O'Grady, Jenifer Ní Ghrádaigh, Niamh Whitfield,

Isobel Henderson, Giollamuire Ó Murchúand, Peter Harbison, Con Manning, Rachel Moss, Michael Ryan, Tim O'Neill, James White, Nancy Dunn-Czak, Dorothy Kelly, Raymond Keaveney, Chris Corlett, Margaret Quinlan and Patrick Maher. The archivists and librarians in Dublin have been most helpful in our research, especially Siobhan Fitzpatrick (Royal Irish Academy), Nessa O'Connor (National Museum of Ireland), Seamus Helferty and the staff at the University College Dublin archives and the archives of the National Museum. As always, the interlibrary loan staff at Eastern Illinois University is endlessly supportive, even from abroad. Kathleen James-Chakraborty also invited me to visit the Françoise Henry reading room in the Art History Department of UCD.

The 1950 diaries and the historical photographs would not have been found without the enthusiasm of Sharon Greene-Douglas to share the materials she had used in her doctoral research, along with the open welcome and willing assistance of Conor McDermott and other staff at the UCD School of Archaeology to study, scan and reproduce them.

I would also like to especially thank Barbara Wright for her transcription of the original French and her indefatigable research efforts during our collaboration to help untangle the references in the text.

Research support funding was provided by Eastern Illinois University's Council on Faculty Research and College of Arts and Humanities. Publication of the photographic illustrations was made possible by a grant from the Heritage Council's Heritage Education, Community and Outreach Grant Scheme 2012. Finally, the Long Room Hub Visiting Research Fellows Programme at Trinity College Dublin provided me the opportunity to work in Dublin while completing this project.

Abbreviations

AD	Anno Domini
BC	Before Christ
BCE	Before the Common Era
CE	The Common Era
FHC	Françoise Henry Collection
IMEC	Institut Mémoires de l'Edition Contemporaine
IVRLA	Irish Virtual Research Library and Archive
JRSAI	*Journal of the Royal Society of Antiquaries of Ireland*
NMI	National Museum of Ireland
OPW	Office of Public Works
PRIA	*Proceedings of the Royal Irish Academy*
RIA	Royal Irish Academy
RSAI	Royal Society of Antiquaries of Ireland
TCD	Trinity College Dublin
UCD	University College Dublin

Introduction

These journals of Françoise Henry were a serendipitous find in the Royal Irish Academy in April 2010 when the eruption of Icelandic volcanoes caused an ash cloud that grounded flights and caused the cancellation of an academic conference at the National University of Ireland, Maynooth, at which I was due to present. Since my own flight from the United States managed to get through, I found myself in Dublin for a few days and decided to see the archival materials that are held at University College Dublin and the Royal Irish Academy on Françoise Henry. I was working on a monographic study of the twentieth-century Zodiaque publications on Romanesque art, for which Françoise Henry wrote three important volumes that expanded the series to earlier medieval art. Because of her connections to both early medieval art and modern artists, she was in a unique position to fully understand the visual relationships that the series was meant to feature. One of the chapters in my book covers key authors, and so I applied for a residential fellowship at Trinity College Dublin in their newly inaugurated humanities research centre, next to the famous Long Room library, called the 'Long Room Hub'. I was subsequently invited to work there and went in June 2011.

During my brief survey of Françoise Henry's papers in 2010, I was at the RIA on 28 April and as I opened folders to take a quick inventory of what papers might be useful for the Zodiaque chapter, I came across a manila envelope containing four small notebooks in which Henry had kept a personal account of her activities in Co. Mayo during 1937–8. Unstructured and quixotic records of her experiences, they are separate from her formal notes for the archaeological report. Three are in French and one, the legend of the Naomhóg as told to her by Miss Cronin, is in English. The first passage I came across was about three boys rowing her in a currach to Inishkea North. Her description of the water, the sky and the people was so lively and evocative that I immediately felt I had found something special. I sent an email with a couple of excerpted phrases to an emerita colleague of French whom I had just met through a mutual acquaintance, sitting in her office at Trinity College only a few blocks away. I asked her if she wanted to walk over and see these enchanting texts for herself. She did, and thus the idea came to me to suggest we work on them together. This was Professor Barbara Wright (Trinity College Dublin) who, living right there in Dublin, was able to transcribe the French texts the following December and found a recent student of French studies, Huw Duffy, to do a translation for us while we both worked on previously committed projects. We then worked with Huw to edit and revise the translation and we visited the Mullet in Co. Mayo during May 2011 to interview local people, many descendants of Inishkea residents, as we tried to tease out the meanings of some of Henry's references. While working at Trinity College in June 2011, I realized there were more of Henry's personal journal pages, from 1946, online from the UCD library archive. We quickly went to work on those and discovered that they resolved a few of the mysteries from the earlier entries. Then it was a matter of finding photographs to correspond to the descriptions in Henry's text – and, though mostly unidentified, there is a rich collection in the School of Archaeology. One can imagine my excitement, after visualizing the stories I had come to know so well as Françoise Henry told them, to open envelopes of small, unidentified snapshots and realize I was able to recognize scenes from 1937–8: Sarah Lavelle on the beach with her seaweed fork; the swan with the broken wing; even 'Dick', the little gull. I was convinced that Henry must have also kept notebooks on her final visit in 1950 and on that same day at the School of Archaeology, they were shown to me. I now had all the materials and only had to return to the Mullet Peninsula during good weather to try to get to the island myself. Over the weekend of 18–19 June, that was finally possible and I was able to meet more local residents who helped me to identify people in the photographs.

Professor Wright is publishing the French transcription with an introductory essay about Henry's prose in *Françoise Henry, Les îles d'Inishkea: carnets personnels* (Lille, 2012). Her introduction focuses on the French text and explores more of the regional history – any reader who is interested in the original prose will be interested in this publication as well. Most of the explanatory notes from archival sources or personal interviews are shared between both publications.

* * *

We feel that these journals represent a special place captured at a special time – the people and the landscape of the Mullet Peninsula and the Inishkea, Duvillaun and Achill islands – beginning just after the residents of the Inishkeas had been moved to the mainland and only a handful of people remained. Françoise Henry's wonderment at this new world she had discovered in the

1 Sample page from Françoise Henry's journal for 12–14 August 1946
(from UCD library archives, FHC: http://hdl.handle.net/10151/OB_0001356_AR).

far west of a country she had already come to love is apparent in her beautiful descriptions of seascapes and physiognomies, lobster traps and curious livestock, birds and blowholes, cultural differences and professional arrangements. She used colours and shapes, metaphors and references in a way that powerfully visualizes for us what she saw in these long-ago days at the very western edge of Europe. Her text follows a long tradition in antiquarian accounts of the

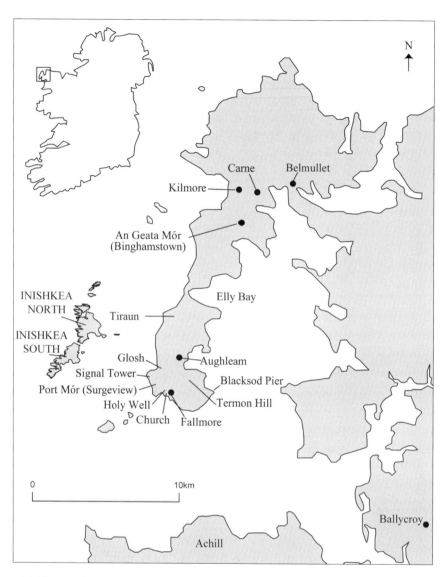

2 Inishkea North is *c.*3km from the Mullet Peninsula at its nearest point. The peninsula has only one commercial centre at Belmullet, where it joins the mainland. The former islanders from Inishkea North lived in a new settlement between Glosh and Surgeview. When Françoise Henry stayed on the Mullet with the Keanes, the house was near Fallmore. In the years when she transferred supplies between the peninsula and the island, the small motor boats most often left from Surgeview, whose pier was called Port Mór. Today, most motor boats leave from Blacksod Pier, as larger boats did in her day, where there is a lighthouse. When the men went back and forth by currach, they often would go straight across to the small beach without a pier at Glosh, but landing was riskier (map prepared by Greg Fennell and Bill Doran).

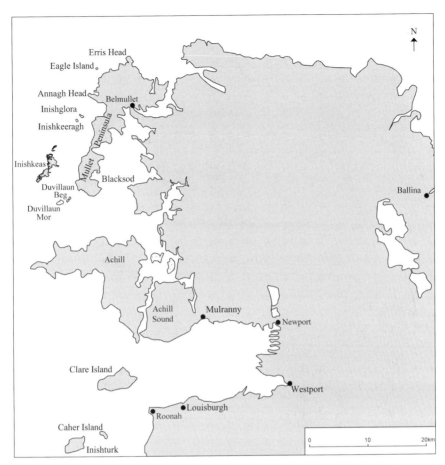

3 Blacksod Bay is bounded on the west by the large and small islands of Duvillaun and on the south by Achill, the only island joined to the mainland by a bridge. Caher Island is to the south of Achill, reached by Françoise Henry via currach from Roonah. Because she needed to retake some photographs here, she first stayed in Louisburgh in 1946 before gathering supplies and launching her expedition from Achill that year, only stopping at the Mullet to pick up workers (map prepared by Greg Fennell and Bill Doran).

Irish islands.[1] Drawn to Early Christian remains, as had been many historians before her, Henry records places that had become symbolic in Ireland of the remote and untainted Gaelic past, free from Anglo-Norman incursions. For her, an educated Frenchwoman, the wild natural environment she so loved

[1] Aidan O'Sullivan, 'The western islands: Ireland's Atlantic islands and the forging of Gaelic Irish national identities' in Noble et al. (eds), *Scottish odysseys: the archaeology of islands* (Stroud, Gloucestershire, 2008), pp 172–90.

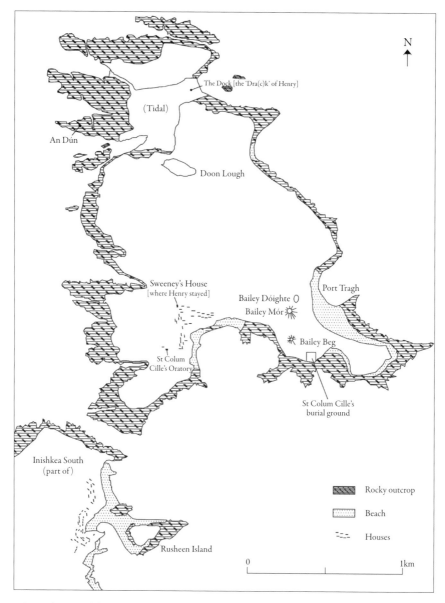

4 Arrivals at Inishkea North are usually made at one of the two small beaches near the village to the south of the island, though Françoise Henry refers to landings at Port Tragh on the eastern edge nearer the Bailey Mór. Henry stayed in a house at the top of the village owned by the Sweeney who transferred her with workers and supplies to the island in 1946. To the far north of the island are Doon Lough, the Dun and the Dock, where Henry often walked when she wanted to get away and think, noting the presence of birds and visiting the swans and seals (map prepared by Greg Fennell and Bill Doran).

was parallel to people who must have seemed as odd to her as she did to them. Many of her workers were illiterate, spoke only Irish, told fantastic folktales and demonstrated superstitious beliefs. There is a bit of the anthropologist in Henry's account of them, but we also know from her research notes that she had read some late nineteenth-century antiquarian descriptions, such as those of T.J. Westropp on the Aran Islands, which linked ancient artefacts with contemporary islanders' lifestyle as if they represented an unbroken historical tradition.

Henry came from a milieu in the early twentieth century where pre-industrialized life was being rediscovered as 'natural'. Growing out of attitudes born by colonialism in the nineteenth century, but now assimilated into literary and artistic movements, people from places like Paris sought 'simpler', even 'primitive', lifestyles to observe and copy. Henry thus felt both an attraction to the inhabitants of regional areas in Ireland even as she apparently diverged from them.

Françoise Henry was born in Paris in 1902. Surrounded by paintings hung in her grandparents' home and the legacy of her grandfather, the art historian Charles Clément, she became interested in studying the history of art for her academic degrees.[2] She trained at the École du Louvre and the Sorbonne, where her interest in early Irish arts incorporated the specializations of her mentors – Emile Mâle (medieval iconography) and his successor Henri Focillon (medieval sculptural forms) as well as Henri Hubert and Salomon Reinach on archaeology and prehistoric excavation, André Michel and Robert Rey on Celtic history. Henry's doctoral theses were on Early Christian Irish art and prehistoric art in Burgundy (*La sculpture Irlandaise pendant les douze premiers siècles de l'ère chrétienne*, under the direction of Focillon in 1932 and *Les tumulus du département de la Côte d'Or* for Henri Hubert in 1933). These studies established Henry as an expert on very early forms of sculptural decoration in stone, metal and enamel. She also had close friends who were contemporary artists exploring abstraction and shared their appreciation for the elemental shapes and patterns that underlie all visual forms, later connecting this to her academic work, saying

2 For more details of Françoise Henry's biography, see Hilary Richardson, 'Henry, Françoise' in the *Dictionary of Irish biography* (Cambridge & Dublin, 2009; http://dib.cambridge.org); Lee Sorensen (ed.), 'Henry, Françoise', *Dictionary of art historians*, http://www.dictionaryofarthistorians.org/henryf.htm; introductions to the three Pindar Press vols cited above from 1983–5, along with attendant bibliography in vol. 3, and the obituaries of Henry by Cecil Curle and Eileen Kane in *JRSAI*, 112 (1982), 142–6. There is also an earlier article and a bibliography written while Henry was still alive in *Studies: An Irish Quarterly Review of Letters, Philosophy and Science*, 64 (1975), 307 ff.

Irish art is not merely an essential record of one particular phase of an obscure past. Apart from historical considerations, it stands out as the most satisfying and most perfect form of non-representational art which Europe has ever known, and because of this it is of immediate and burning interest for the artists of our time.[3]

Henry had also trained in drawing and her ability to sketch records of the objects and decoration that she found working in the field served her well as she made adept relationships between the designs found on stone, metal and painted vellum. One of Henry's greatest contributions to the field of art history lies in the wide-ranging survey she made of early arts from Ireland, Britain, Scandinavia and France with a view to tracing the origins of many motifs in Ireland that also appeared across Western Europe. With Irish monks going abroad to study or to teach, as well as non-Irish coming to study in Irish monasteries, disentangling the layers of exchange was a monumental task.

Françoise Henry was particularly taken by Henri Focillon's ideas about sculptural form; notions which must have paralleled discussions by the contemporaries that she would have heard in artistic circles in Paris during the 1930s. Two kinds of topics may have caught her ear while working on ancient Celtic and Early Christian artefacts. One concerned the role of modern artists and the Church. Since the nineteenth century, religious subjects had been portrayed in a naturalistic fashion modelled upon late Renaissance and early baroque Italian models. Piety was conveyed through a saccharine style often called 'Saint Sulpicean' due to its ubiquitous appearance among religious objects sold in small shops around the church of St Sulpice in Paris (now mostly easily found at pilgrimage sites like Lourdes).[4] The emptiness of this work was called out at the end of the century by artists, such as the Nabis, who tried to find a more profound and expressive way to instil spiritual content in painting.

The Nabis were followed by artists working in collaborative modern decoration such as by Bonnard, Rouault, Léger, Matisse, Braque, Chagall and others on the church at Assy, Matisse's chapel at Vence, or Le Corbusier's Ronchamp and La Tourette. These works met strong resistance among Catholics and caused sensational debate in art circles. They concerned the other strain of contemporary art theory that would have surrounded Henry in the 1930s – the then more than twenty-year-old discourse on the superiority of abstraction and non-representational compositions.

3 Françoise Henry, *Early Christian Irish art* (Cork, 1954, 3rd ed., 1979), p. 16.   4 Daniel Mitsui, 'Scylla & Charybdis: l'art Saint-Sulpice & l'art sacré', *The lion & the cardinal*, 20 June 2009 [http://www.danielmitsui.

For example, although there was more than one school of 'Cubism', adherents had attempted to understand and convey the inherent structure of objects. A contemporary painter who served as an early apologist for the revaluation of pre-gothic medieval art along these lines was Albert Gleizes. He wrote about art and spirituality, using ancient and medieval examples to support his belief that simpler forms within sophisticated compositions, free of elaborate representational conceits, could offer profound meditative vehicles for viewers. In his book *Vers une conscience plastique: la forme et l'histoire*,[5] he includes illustrations that break down familiar artworks into their essential structural and rhythmic lines. A few examples even show his awareness of early Irish art.

Focillon's approach to medieval sculpture would have resonated within these contemporary discussions of abstraction.[6] His interest in medieval architectural decoration did not follow the Classical and text-bound focus of his predecessor, Emile Mâle, who interpreted the meaning of narrative scenes with iconographic analyses. Rather, Focillon saw the execution of visual scenes by medieval sculptors as a formal technical challenge to extract forms, even the very spirit of the era's art, from within blocks of stone. He believed in the strata of styles, one succeeding the other in cyclical fashion. In this, he was influenced by modernist interest in the reduction of complex design to essential geometric compositions.

Focillon attempted to record the process of medieval sculpture by following the shapes into which designs were cut. In fact, his closest student, Jurgis Baltrusaitis, employed his teacher's method in a comprehensive study of Romanesque capitals.[7] The way that the illustrative line drawings convey the essential shapes, flattening the volumes and simplifying the narrative details, added to the simultaneously modernist and primitive appreciation for Romanesque art. But Focillon did not value Irish art beyond its role among many precursors for European Romanesque art. Françoise Henry saw more to it and took it as her primary subject, using his notion of stylistic strata to help date her archaeological finds. She separated periods not only by historical watershed events, such as the arrival of Christian missionaries or Viking invaders, but also by their 'spirit', quoting Focillon's description of medieval Irish art as 'one of the most astonishing of human reveries, one of the most mysterious caprices of the intellect'.[8] She set out to decode that mystery through careful

com/hieronymus/index.blog/1839802/scylla-charybdis-lart-saintsulpice-lart-sacre]   5 Albert Gleizes, *Vers une conscience plastique, la forme et l'histoire* (Paris, 1932).   6 See Focillon's landmark study *La vie des formes* (Paris, 1939), but also Henry's own testimonial to him in 'Henri Focillon', *Studies in Early Christian and medieval Irish art, vol. ii: manuscript illumination* (London, 1984), pp 1–10.   7 Jurgis Baltrusaitis, *La stylistique ornementale dans la sculpture romane* (Paris, 1931).   8 Henry, 'Henri Focillon',

analyses of primary textual sources, applying what she had learned from Mâle, as she was exploring the artefacts excavated from prehistoric and early medieval sites. This double focus allowed her to make careful alignments between peoples, events and objects in a fresher way than had been approached by most native Irish up until that time. Adopting Focillon's critical eye to form and affected by her close friendships with contemporary artists, such as the Irish abstract painter Mainie Jellett (1897–1944), who also happened to be a student of Gleizes, Françoise Henry analyzed and followed the appearance of visual motifs on various media more closely than others in her field, such as Arthur Kingsley Porter.

After publishing his important works on Romanesque art, including the interchange of sculptors across the pilgrimage roads of France and Spain,[9] Porter became interested in Celtic art during the late 1920s. A Harvard professor with a wealthy wife, he purchased a castle at Glenveagh in northwest Ireland and spent his time between academic terms there and in a small cottage he built on Inishbofin, an island off the coast of Co. Donegal. He also appreciated Irish art as a 'harbinger of the Romanesque', but depended mostly upon what he already knew from other visual art to explain the mysteries of the iconography, whereas Henry worked more deliberately to relate all Irish examples and relevant literary sources. For instance, he acknowledged her better references in Christian scenes for Ulster crosses in his *corrigenda* to *The crosses and culture of Ireland* (New Haven, 1931) after reading the article in which she took this distinguished scholar to task for ignoring larger photographic resources than his own, for not working systematically and chronologically on all Irish crosses but just picking and choosing scenes he could recognize, for not putting together logical groupings of scenes, for not looking at other media of art with similar ornamentation and for looking only to models in the 'Orient', such as Byzantium or Coptic Egypt, when he could not show the same influence in England, rather than also closer to hand in Carolingian ivories from the west of the European continent (*Revue archéologique*, ser. 5, vol. 32:2 (1930), 89–109). Henry was only 28 when she wrote this tough critique of Porter's theories, a doctoral student. It is a masterful example of the detailed method of study she would pursue throughout her life and the importance of her substantial contributions to the field heralded by scholars both in and out of Ireland.[10]

p. 4; Henry, *Early Christian Irish art*, p. 13.   9 Arthur Kingsley Porter, *Romanesque sculpture of the pilgrimage roads* (Boston, 1923).   10 Henry's lifelong claim of Carolingian sources for Irish art has since been challenged, most notably by Roger Stalley, who prefers her suggestions of Early Christian models ('European art and Irish high crosses', *PRIA*, 90C (1990), 135–58, also available at http://www.jstor.org/stable/25516066), but her methods of analysis were essential for further progress in this field of study.

5 Fallmore cemetery showing grave with type of weathered cross and large white pebbles that Henry mentions. One wall of the ruin of St Deirbhile's Church is in the background (photograph by Janet Marquardt, May 2011).

6 Early Medieval stone slab on Inishkea North (photograph by Françoise Henry; all photographs in this book are by Françoise Henry unless stated otherwise).

7 Current condition of Early Medieval stone slab on Inishkea North. This is the same slab photographed by Françoise Henry during her excavations – see above (photograph by Janet Marquardt, June 2011).

8 Early Medieval stone slab on Inishkea North (photograph by Janet Marquardt, June 2011).

Françoise Henry had already travelled the Irish landscape with the friend who first interested her in the country in 1926, Carrie Fitzgerald, and Marie Duport.[11] Beginning with the area around Cashel, Co. Tipperary, in Fitzgerald's little red sports car, her first visit resulted in her first article, a study of Cormac's Chapel at Cashel and her photographs of the stone crosses – such as the ones that particularly struck her at Ahenny – led to her principal thesis with Focillon. The latter was published in Paris in 1933, then revised and translated into English in 1940 for the London publication entitled *Irish art in the Early Christian period* (as a companion volume to T.D. Kendrick's *Anglo-Saxon art*). Her research for this was funded by grants from the Sorbonne and the International Federation of University Women. She would go on to study the early sculpture and manuscripts all over Ireland and initiate or join excavations in Scotland, Scandinavia and France as well as Irish sites such as Glendalough (Wicklow), the Aran Islands and Cashel – along with Inishkea North. She was part of a former Focillon student threesome: her friend Cecil Curle and her cousin Genevieve Micheli also worked on Early Christian European arts and we can find them thanking each other in early publications. Henry

11 Marie Duport, 'La sculpture irlandaise à fin du Moyen Age', *La revue de l'art ancien et moderne*, 66 (1934), 49–62.

9 Early Medieval stone slab on Inishkea North (photograph by Janet Marquardt, June 2011).

10 View of the Bailey Mór (photograph by Janet Marquardt, June 2011).

dedicated *Irish art in the Early Christian period* to Curle and Micheli 'in remembrance of our common researches'. In *Antiquity* (1936), Curle writes that she is greatly indebted to Mlle Henry for help in writing her first paper, on the St Andrews Sarcophagus and the Nigg cross-slab. Henry and Curle co-authored 'Early Christian art in Scotland' for the *Gazette des Beaux-Arts* (1943), and in 1950 Henry thanks Micheli for help with her article 'Les débuts de la miniature irlandaise' in the same journal.

In 1937, Henry went to Inishkea twice to photograph the remains of St Columba's Church and five cross-slabs.[12] Henry then requested and was granted permission to excavate by the Office of Public Works at Duvillaun and Inishkea North in May 1938 for three months from 1 June.[13] The licence specified that her 'finds would be disposed of as directed by the National Museum'. In the event, Henry stayed on Inishkea North only until 11 July, excavating a sand dune, the Bailey Mór, and lightly exploring the upper part of a shell and bone pile nearer the shore on the eastern side of the island as well as the area near the cemetery. On the Bailey Mór, she uncovered the remains of three houses

---

12 Françoise Henry, 'Remains of the Early Christian period on Inishkea North, Co. Mayo', *JRSAI*, 75:3 (1945), 127–55. 13 There are two excavation licences for 1938: one for Duvillaun Mór and one for Inishkea North. There is one 1946 licence for Inishkea North.

11 One of the excavated houses on the Bailey Mór
(photograph by Janet Marquardt, June 2011).

in 1938, one oblong and two beehive stone constructions, and identified six others along with numerous unnamed buildings.[14] She traced their outlines and recorded the stratification layers of the remains, especially around the hearths. She also found skeletons and some basic household utensils, along with a few personal items including a bone comb. She dated the settlement between the sixth and tenth centuries CE (up to the Viking invasions), definitively assigning it a monastic purpose and relating it to other early monastic sites found on islands, with the cross-slabs being late seventh or early eighth century.[15]

Henry returned to Inishkea North to continue excavation of the Bailey Mór in 1946, when important material finds convinced her of the value of another dig in 1950, on which she published two articles.[16] One continued

---

14 Henry knew of the beehive structures on Skellig Michael from Dunraven's late nineteenth-century publications, and published her own article on them in 1948: 'Early Irish monasteries, boat-shaped oratories and beehive huts', *County Louth Archaeological Journal*, 11:4 (1948), 296–304. Dunraven's editor was Margaret Stokes, who herself studied and wrote on Irish art. She is often mentioned as a sort of foremother of Françoise Henry.   **15** This dating has since been revised by Peter Harbison. See his essay in Etienne Rynne (ed.), *Figures from the past: studies on figurative art in Christian Ireland in honour of Helen M. Roe* (Dublin, 1987), pp 73–91.   **16** Françoise Henry, 'New monuments from Inishkea North, Co. Mayo', *JRSAI*, 81 (1951), 65–9; Françoise Henry, 'A wooden hut on Inishkea North, Co. Mayo (Site 3, House A)',

the description of the large cross-slabs begun in 1937–8 and 1946, asserting that stone carving had clearly been important during the Early Christian period on the Inishkeas and listing some of the key design features. The second article recorded the discovery of a purple dye manufacturing facility on a second sand mound, near the Bailey Mór, as well as a bronze brooch and bronze handle, the latter perhaps originally belonging to a mirror.

As Henry herself stated, these were the first systematic excavations of an Early Christian monastery with the beehive type structure.[17] Sharon Greene-Douglas, who has worked on assembling a full record of Henry's Inishkea excavations as part of her study of the history of settlements on the islands in Co. Mayo,[18] believes that although Henry's records were not comprehensive, it is clear she relied upon her memory for the parts that were written up:

> Henry was essentially on her own as regards the excavation. The men working for her would have had no experience of this kind of work and it is questionable how much they understood of what exactly she was trying to do. They did the 'heavy' work, including moving large amounts of sand, while she alone had the responsibility of recording as they worked. It is no wonder that some of the records are incomplete, as she was trying to keep up with their digging ... It is important to note the confidence with which she embarked on this ambitious project also – and the confidence of the 'powers that be' in her ability to carry it out. She was clearly a capable archaeologist, despite the fact that we tend to remember her as an art historian. As well as the excavation conditions, the failures of her recording techniques reflect also on the recording techniques of the early twentieth century, when modern archaeology was still somewhat in its infancy. However, she must also be applauded for her approach to the environmental evidence. She had all the bird and animal bones identified in an attempt to understand the diet of the islanders. She collected burnt cereal grains ... and charcoal samples ... which has allowed for them to be recently identified ... and radiocarbon dated. She was thorough when it came to collecting artefacts (including things like manufacturing debris), even if she did not always record exact provenances. She also put together a large catalogue of all the quern stones she found on the island, including sketches, measurements and

JRSAI, 82:2 (1952), 163–78. 17 Henry, 'Remains of the Early Christian period on Inishkea North', 154.
18 S.A. Greene, 'Settlement, identity & change on the Atlantic islands of north-west Co. Mayo, AD400–1200' (PhD, UCD, 2009).

12 Men installing posts for protective perimeter fence around excavation area on top of the Bailey Mór.

photographs. Her survey of early monastic and other stone dwellings on the Ivereagh Peninsula and Valentia Island, Co. Kerry, which she carried out between 1937 and 1954,[19] was important in establishing that not all beehive huts were necessarily the result of ecclesiastical (or indeed eremitic, as believed at the end of the previous century) settlement.[20] The survey also allowed for her comparison of the Inishkea beehives to a number of other examples in the west of Ireland.[21] She could be called a pioneer of modern archaeological research into the early ecclesiastical sites of the west of Ireland.[22]

Greene's own interpretation, in the context of modern archaeological scholarship and research, has shown that the settlement developed into an important ecclesiastical site by the eighth century CE, probably a pilgrimage destination. Even more interesting is that, from around the beginning of the ninth century, the character of the settlement completely changed and the monastery became a secular Scandinavian settlement. Scandinavian evidence

19 Françoise Henry, 'Early monasteries, beehive huts, and dry-stone houses in the neighbourhood of Caherciveen and Waterville (Co. Kerry)', *PRIA*, 58:3 (1957), 45–166.   20 Ibid., 45.   21 Henry, 'Remains of the Early Christian period on Inishkea North', 148.   22 Email from Sharon Greene-Douglas to the author,

from the west coast is rare and still poorly understood, and without Henry's excavations one of the important pieces of evidence would be missing, as such large-scale excavations on offshore islands are still rare.

Roaming pastured animals, particularly cows and donkeys, caused damage during the excavation, and Henry had to request supplies to fence off the area.[23] Then removal of archaeological artefacts from the island for the National Museum caused local consternation. Although Irish heritage had gained momentum since the days of George Petrie's romantic documentation in the nineteenth century and the rise of nationalism after the success of the movement toward Irish independence, there was not yet a strong sense of the benefits of centralized conservation. As well, local people had long attributed religious importance to these Early Christian remains and considered the ground, along with the monumental decorated stones, to be sacred.[24] A precedent had been set, however, in the early 1930s, by a team of archaeologists from Harvard University, under Kingsley Porter, who found and conveyed to the National Museum a large number of historical objects. The issue for Henry's Inishkea North excavation concerned which land was considered to belong to the government. Harold Leask, Office of Public Works, wrote to her on 2 June 1938 that

> all the burial spots on the island – from St Columba's Church upwards – are not in the hands of the tenant-purchasers but in those of the state itself ... This good news means that no local person has any right to finds, if any be made.

Nevertheless, it appears that at first John Reilly, then living on Inishkea North, barred the loading of some of the large stones for removal (per letter of Mary Keane to Henry, 19 July 1938). A letter from Ann Cawley on 28 July 1938 indicated that the local priest at Blacksod gave a sermon on Sunday 24 July telling the congregation about Henry's work and asserting that the stones belonged in the National Museum for protection. Ann Cawley felt that would

---

16 June 2011, regarding her assessment of Henry's excavation records. **23** For instance, see letters to Henry regarding arrangements for supplies from Harold Leask of 1 and 2 July and to McIntyre & Co. Stores in Belmullet of 2 July 1938. These letters all referenced here are conserved in the Françoise Henry Collection of the Irish Virtual Research Library and Archive at UCD [http://hdl.handle.net/10151/OB_0001356_AR]. Footnotes that reference page numbers come from the subentries under her collections for Stone/Sites/Notes relating to the excavations at Inishkea, Co. Mayo. **24** One can see in the journal text for 20 September 1937 that Henry refers to the superstitions of the postmistress about saintly relics when she tries to mail some bones that she has excavated.

resolve any further action and allow John Padden, the boatman who most often carried Henry and her supplies to/from the island, to transport them away to the peninsula. However, this did not end the problem and the stones were not removed from the island until 1939, when police were sent to protect them from local intervention.

Adolf Mahr, the director of the National Museum, who had been involved in granting permission for the Harvard digs, wrote to Henry that he was not especially keen to remove the monumental stones from their original setting, but felt that at least one would justify the funds extended to her.[25] He also understood her concerns that they were too vulnerable to damage *in situ*. He wrote to Henry on 7 July 1938:

> I agree with you wholeheartedly that field monuments should remain where they are, but I gather that in the present case you are yourself rather of the opinion that the three slabs had better be put in a safe place in the Museum. I realize quite well that it is very awkward for you to have to make all these preparations for transport etc., but as you are seemingly willing to do so, and as from what you say it appears to be the best course to adopt, I take your hint and act accordingly to your suggestions.[26]

Henry was not insensitive to the local religious beliefs in spite of her higher education and Protestant upbringing. She loved the Catholic faith, as can be evidenced by her study of Irish Christian art and even her notes about saints and legends in these journals, and she eventually converted. But she also cared about the deterioration of the ancient art she was uncovering and sometimes believed the museum the best place for conservation. She had begun her interest in Irish art with monumental crosses and decorated slabs and whenever she went to a new area, she prepared with notes on the stone slabs as recorded in articles by H.S. Crawford from 1912–16.[27] She was able to publish images of some from both Duvillaun and Inishkea North that he had not included,[28] as well as one from Tarmon, on the Mullet, that was unknown altogether.[29] It is clear that she cared a great deal about the preservation of these artworks.

Françoise Henry's personal journals translated here were begun in 1937, the year she first went to the Mullet Peninsula in Co. Mayo to investigate the

---

25 Handwritten note added to letter from Mahr to Henry dated 21 June 1938 and point repeated again in one dated 28 June 1938.   26 Gerry Mullins, *Dublin Nazi No. 1: the life of Adolf Mahr* (Dublin, 2007), pp 39–40.   27 These can all be found in *JRSAI*.   28 Françoise Henry, 'Early Christian slabs and pillar stones in the West of Ireland', *JRSAI*, 6/2 (1937), 265–79; see pls 29 and 33.   29 Ibid., 330–1 and pl. 31.

possibility of excavating at the Inishkeas. The entries do not regularly appear for every day and are not meant as an official record. They are simply her notes and impressions of a place and a people very far and very different from the life she knew in France. At times, she can be quite blunt about her impressions, frustrations or fears. Some of Henry's characterizations of people can be read as unflattering. She uses a very metaphorical and descriptive prose that borders upon exaggeration and caricature at times, but which also shows a great deal of affection for the people with whom she worked. One assumes these private notes and nicknames helped her keep track of the many people she met, especially since she did not speak Irish as a native would and names might have been difficult to retain. However, her descriptive prose is quite beautiful in the original French, vividly evoking the wild beauty of far western Ireland in an original style. We have tried to capture her meaning in this English translation to the best of our ability to understand references to contemporary practices, French idioms and local history. Sometimes she was just jotting down a short informational note or using quick abbreviations, so the text has required some investigation to produce. The journals for 1937/8 and 1946 are written in French with occasional phrases in English and Irish. The daybooks for 1950, from which we excerpted entries, are in English. It is said, by those who knew her, that Henry spoke English well but always retained a strong French accent. She attended Irish classes while staying in Connemara during 1928 and her archives at the UCD library include a little booklet entitled *Irish in a month*.[30] Certainly her friendship with Maureen O'Daly (Máirín Bean Uí Dhálaigh), whom we see accompanying her to the island, and who worked on the *Dictionary of the Irish language*, would also have been helpful in this regard.

Henry found lodging in 1937 in Fallmore, at the tip of the Mullet peninsula, with a couple, Stephan and Mary Keane, who ran a small grocery store and offered rooms.[31] The house, 'Sea View', is still in place, though the small western addition that held the store and lodging rooms has been removed. Many of the places she visited on her walks along the southern roads of this bay are also still extant – the cemetery with its eroded crosses and ruined church, the holy well, the Napoleonic tower at Glosh, a bit of the pier at Surgeview/Port Mór

30 From the chronology of Françoise Henry's life prepared by Giollamuire Ó Murchúand (son of Henry's friends Máirín and Domhnall O'Murchadha), unpublished, p. 2. The Irish language booklet can be found at http://hdl.handle.net/10151/OB_0001356_AR, images 221–246.   31 Grocery receipts from the Keane store show that Henry purchased basic supplies such as matches, candles, tea, soap, flour, milk, cheese, oil, salt, potatoes, onions, tinned vegetables/legumes, preserved or tinned meats, eggs, fruits, paper, postage stamps and cigarettes (once noted as a packet per day for Ann Cawley, but we know that Henry herself also smoked). She also had a bicycle transported to Fallmore from Dublin for local use.

from where she embarked and returned to the mainland, the Bailey Mór where she excavated and the house in which she lived on Inishkea North, which had been abandoned only two or three years earlier, when the islanders were moved off the islands by the government.[32] Those islanders who did not emigrate to England or the United States were given houses with four- or five-acre plots in Fallmore and Glosh. It was among them that Henry found men to hire for her excavations and transport and the woman, Ann Cawley, who came as her cook and housekeeper. This would have been the first time most, if not all, of these men encountered a female 'boss', which may account for some of the struggles between them and Henry. Naturally we are reading only her side of the labour dissatisfactions in these pages and must be aware that she may, at times, have been unfair in her judgments of the men. They doubtless saw her as impatient and demanding, working in a different kind of rhythm more akin to the driven city professional than the lives of fishermen and others dependent upon the seasons and natural elements for their livelihood. In fact, Henry was on a very small budget for the Inishkea excavation work, thus impelling her to demand much of her workers. Henry's work kept her in Dublin, where she moved among people with similar levels of education and culture as her own. Though she studied the Irish language, travelled to remote locations and made research into the early history of Irish art and culture her lifelong career, her journal texts demonstrate that she retained many urban perspectives in surveying the rural scene. Her budget was limited by small grants from the RIA,[33] but the employment was welcome to the community and 'Miss Henry' is generally well remembered by the folk who heard their grandparents talk about her or were children during her later visit in 1950.

The history of the Mullet and the islands is rich and easily found in fuller studies such as Brian Dornan's *Mayo's lost islands: the Inishkeas* (Dublin, 2000) or Rita Nolan, *Within the Mullet* (Naas, 3rd ed. 2000). Legends to which references can be found, especially that of the *Naomhóg*, appear in multiple forms, such as T.H. White, *The Godstone and the Blackymor* (London, 1959). Archival materials held in UCD (available online at http://hdl.handle.net/10151/OB_0001356_AR), the RIA and the NMI include letters between Henry and administrators regarding her excavation work and the fate of the objects she found, plus receipts she kept for her expenses – including her supply

---

32 Note that many people of the Mullet Peninsula still refer to the islands as home – thus the term used for going 'to' the islands is to go 'in', while heading to the mainland at Blacksod Bay is considered going 'out'.   33 Letter from Harold Leask at the National Museum dated 2 June 1938 mentions an allocation of twenty pounds from the RIA's Excavation Committee.

purchases and worker pay cheques. The pages of the 1946 diary are scanned and available at that site as well. There is also an archive of photographs that she left to UCD in the School of Archaeology.

Françoise Henry kept a country home in Burgundy, at Lindry ('Les Bretons'), even while teaching in Dublin, and spent most holidays there, often inviting her Irish friends and students to visit. Her appointment at UCD began in 1932 when she was invited to lecture in French. There was no art history programme, and little interest in Irish art, but in 1934 she was invited to give a Purser–Griffith series of lectures that grew into a regular course on the history of European painting.[34] She took this broader application of art history very seriously and travelled in Europe to learn more for her lectures, especially in Italy, in order to bring a wide range of Continental examples to her teaching. By 1948, Henry's publications on her Irish excavations earned her an appointment in the Department of Celtic Archaeology, where we know she was teaching courses on Celtic art in 1959.[35] In 1965, an honours degree in the History of European Painting was established at UCD and Henry was made its Director of Special Studies. Her intense interest in early Irish art coincided with the enthusiasm of colleagues for Celtic literature and history – texts of which she availed herself when decoding the art – and she was instrumental in introducing the idea to study both art history for a degree and Irish art as a subject at university level.

Henry took leave during the Second World War to work both in London (in a factory) and in France (as an ambulance driver) as well as with the Vaucher Commission (formed to identify important art monuments needing

---

34 The Purser–Griffith lecture series was set up by Sarah Purser, an artist and a governor and guardian of the National Gallery of Ireland from January 1914 until her death in 1943. She was cousin to the wealthy Dame 'Nina' Purser, who married Sir John Griffith; he inherited her estate. Sarah Purser wanted to assuage the difficulty of finding qualified Irish candidates for the National Gallery directorship and decided to approach both TCD and UCD to endow an annual scholarship in the history of European painting. She convinced Senator Griffith to match her sum and devised a two-paper examination in consultation with Thomas Bodkin, then director of the National Gallery. Dr Coffey, UCD president, initiated a lecture course that would prepare students for the exam and asked Henry, who was at the time a lecturer in French, to teach it. In fact, the lectures were offered only at UCD and in the French language for the first years. Though opened as free lectures to all students, those who wished to take the diploma examination had to pay a fee, but were entitled to an additional weekly tutorial. See John O'Grady, *The life and work of Sarah Purser* (Dublin, 1996), pp 136–8. 35 Although Michael Ryan ('David Sweetman: a personal memoir' in Conleth Manning (ed.), *From ringforts to fortified houses: studies on castles and other monuments in honour of David Sweetman* (Bray, Co. Wicklow, 2007), p. ix) claims the archaeology students did not take courses with Henry by his day, her letter to Angelico Surchamp about his gift of *L'art gaulois* in January 1959 states that she was giving courses in Celtic art at that time. It is unlikely these would have been housed with the small history of European painting program (IMEC: 53.1).

protection). In 1947, Henry was awarded a *Chevalier de la Légion d'honneur*, which she lists on a CV in her RIA papers as 'for her scientific work', but which her friend and student, Hilary Richardson, aligns with her war service.[36] It may be that the Vaucher Commission work was the catalyst, which would account for both descriptions. Françoise Henry was one of the first four women elected to the RIA in 1949.

To her students and colleagues, she was always 'Mademoiselle', never Dr Henry. She was well loved by students, who found her combination of rigour and encouragement empowering. In her History of European Painting first-year course, she assigned both Mâle and Focillon,[37] thus perpetuating the balanced approach to art history that had served her so well. Her standards were high – in referring to a textbook rife with errors, she would invariably use 'those creatures' in lieu of the authors' names and was well known to be able to affect deafness if someone's conversation was not worth her time. Her colleagues remember a similar dismissal of 'nonsense', but that she 'wore her learning lightly'[38] and was infinitely generous.

A selected list of Henry's publications must include her collected articles in three volumes: *Studies in Early Christian and medieval Irish art* (London, 1983–5) and the three volumes she produced for the famous Zodiaque publications on Romanesque art (*L'art irlandais*) in 1963–4,[39] of which the English editions from 1965–70 contain more complete supporting documentation. These latter represent some of the most important early volumes for the series 'La nuit des temps', which was organized geographically by region and for which the first two volumes of Henry's Irish contribution served as introductory material, preliminary to the central focus on art from the years 1000–1200. The books were produced by the monastery of La Pierre-qui-Vire in Burgundy and served to both document Romanesque art and bring the religious subject matter out in affordable volumes, but also to reintroduce pre-gothic medieval material to a twentieth-century public with edgy, highly artistic photographs reproduced as rich photogravures designed to appeal to modernist taste. Henry's important texts demonstrated a clear understanding of the connections between early medieval art and the modernist aesthetic that the Zodiaque editor, Angelico Surchamp, was trying to give the collection's photographs. Finally, Henry's knowledge of Irish manuscripts and the relationship of their

36 *Dictionary of Irish biography* entry, see n. 1.   37 Emile Mâle, *The Gothic image: religious art in France of the thirteenth century* (New York, 1958); Henri Focillon, *The art of the West in the Middle Ages* (London, 1963).   38 From the obituary by Eileen Kane, *JRSAI*, 112 (1982), 146.   39 Janet T. Marquardt, *Zodiaque: making medieval modern, 1951–2001* (University Park, PA, forthcoming 2013).

decoration to sculptural forms culminated in her final major publication in Thames and Hudson's first facsimile edition of the *Book of Kells* from 1974. Françoise Henry died on 10 February 1982 and is buried in Lindry, near Auxerre, France.

The form of these journals is unstructured – Henry begins with some short notes in 1937 when she first arrives in Fallmore, recording the people she met and the things they said; the appearance of the striking landscapes and seascapes when she walks on the roads at this tip of the Mullet Peninsula; her impressions attending a wake and burial. After this, she makes it to Inishkea North for the first time and visits some of the remaining residents. The events of 10–11 April end back in Fallmore, where she sees the sunset silhouette of the Inishkeas.

On 12 or 13 April, Henry visits Miss Cronin, who tells her the legend of the *Naomhóg* (recorded in a separate small notebook). Then, on 14 and 15 April, she interacts with local women on the Mullet and on the 17th with people in the Keane house, where she hears the legend of the Children of Lir. Returning to 16 April (pages written out of chronological order), she learns that two local men are going to Scotland for work and listens to a discussion about a sick cow. She again describes the conditions of the sea and the view of Slievemore, on Achill, across the bay. On 18 April, she goes in a currach with three others to the island of Duvillaun Mór.

In September of the same year, a second 1937 notebook begins with a series of cryptic notes about the legend of St Deirbhile, whose church and well are in the cemetery at Fallmore (see colour pl. 14), and St Brendan. Henry has returned to Co. Mayo for another visit to Inishkea North after working with Cecil Curle for the second year at the excavation site in the Brough of Birsay (Orkney Islands, Scotland).[40]

When Henry's journal accounts recommence on 18 September, she is awaiting good weather for crossing to the island, where she apparently digs for two days. She must convince Stephan Keane to get rowers to take her; finally, they are only successful in convincing former Inishkea residents, who take her in a currach. On 20 September, she meets the postmistress, Mrs Sweeney, who is suspicious of the bones, and she prepares to go over to Achill in a currach the following day. The entries end there.

Henry returned to the Mullet in 1938 to begin her formal excavation of Inishkea North. Ann Cawley, who will work for Henry, is introduced to her

---

40 Cecil L. Curle & Françoise Henry, 'Early Christian art in Scotland', *Gazette des Beaux-arts*, ser. 6.24:2 (1943), 257–72. The finds at this location so similar to the western islands of Ireland may have given Henry hope that Inishkea North would yield treasures.

13 Men inspecting Inishkea-type currachs (see p. 35, n. 16).

on 7 June and she begins to negotiate for workers and a transport boat. On 9 June she is taken over with her supplies, Ann, Maureen (O'Daly, the linguist) and three men who will dig – Pat, Seán and Seánín. They have arranged with a former islander for a house in which to live, the last at the top of the road on Inishkea North, and move in. The livestock gather around it. She describes her three male workers. The next day they explore the island and between 11 and 16 June they begin the excavation. Henry records stories told around meals, but nothing about the work itself – *that* she kept for her official excavation report notebooks. There are the sketches, plans, measurements, hypotheses and documentation of finds. Two are extant, as far as this author knows; one for 1938 and one for 1946.[41] In her personal journals, however, she prefers to describe the weather, the landscape, and the behaviour of the people with whom she is working. By 1950, she has changed her method and we find all the material in one place – excavation notes, pay records, personal observations.[42]

41 The 1937/8 personal diaries are in the RIA and the 1946 personal diaries are in the Special Collections department of the UCD library. All the archaeological records are in the School of Archaeology at UCD. 42 These are held by the UCD School of Archaeology, along with photographic and other materials that Dr Henry left to them upon her retirement.

14 Man inspecting Inishkea-type currach (see p. 35, n. 16).

On 18 June 1938, she records some issues that arise with her workers and discussions about their leaving for the weekend; Henry stays and is happy to be alone on the island for the first time. Upon their departure, she walks, engages with the animals, thinks about ghosts and weathers a storm. The following days are spent in observing this striking landscape, the seals and the weather, until the others return with full lobster pots on the 20th.

The entries then skip to Saturday 25 June, when two girls from Inishkea South come to spend the weekend with Henry's party and they find a baby gull and take it inside the house. They have a lively time together in the evening. On 26 June, the girls' father – who had been fishing since Thursday – returns earlier than expected with lobsters, which everyone shares. She starts to worry about supplies and begins to take wood from old currachs for the fire. On 27 June, there is a powerful storm, which halts their work, as well as fishing, so they are all together again and Henry notes the historically communal nature of their arrangement as supplies are shared.

In Henry's 28 June entry, she describes Ann and complains about her a bit as her own frustration begins to show. They go down to the fishermen's house for warmth as there is nothing with which to make a fire in their own. On 29 June, the weather seems to allow work again. They find wood after exploration, and in this entry and that of 30 June, Henry describes Ann's moods and the effect of the men's absences when supplies are wanting.

On 1 July, Henry decides to take a currach by herself to the south island, but ends up going with Seán. Later, in the evening, she scolds those who complain. On 2 July, she begins to wrap up the work, though the men act surprised that she would not be employing them all summer. She describes them at more length. Pat, who has frustrated her, leaves, and sends back Peter, another, younger, son to replace him. On 4 and 5 July, she notes that things are much less stressful without Pat and records some fun everyone has together. Pay sheets are signed and the workers leave while she stays on with Ann. The fishermen leave on 10 and 11 July, then Stephan Keane and some priests come to visit.

There are only thirty handwritten pages from the 1946 notebook, but Henry's text takes us back to the world she introduced in 1937. The entries begin in Louisburgh, near Westport, as she began this trip with a stop on Caher Island in order to re-photograph the remains there. She then goes to Achill and gets her supplies from Sweeney, departing from Achill Sound and, only stopping at the Mullet to pick up Ann and her workmen, she immediately departs for Inishkea North. The journal covers about one month – 3 August to 8 September – during which the weather is rough a great deal of the time, making work on the dig difficult. She has different workers this time round, as well as more contact with some men living on the island.

For the 1950 entries, we have extracted Henry's diary material from her archaeological notes. This year, supplies are collected at Blacksod pier and she again depends upon Ann to find workers. She has some of the same men from previous digs, some new. We learn more about the island's flora, fauna, animals and powerful weather. She struggles to manage labour, food supplies and personalities. As always, she seeks solace in the fascinating and rugged landscape she found at Inishkea North.

Janet T. Marquardt
10 February 2012

The journals

What follows is the text of seven of Françoise Henry's personal notebooks from 1937–8, 1946 and 1950. The first four larger notebooks are written almost entirely in French and in ink, with occasional small sections in pencil. A smaller one, in pencil, records a legend she was told, in English (pp 41–3). The two from 1950 are also primarily in English. We have used square brackets to complete text when she abbreviated words and for translations of the few Irish words that appear and which we have left in this transcription. Any discrepancies from the French text or problematic translations are explained in the footnotes, as well as local and historical references.

All dates have been regularized from Henry's various styles. Her occasional misspellings have been corrected. We have also regularized the spelling of 'currach', 'Colum Cille', 'Duvillaun' and 'beg' and other commonly used terms and names. Words that she hyphenated, now more commonly spelled as single words, have been changed. Except when Henry uses AD or BC, we have used CE or BCE. When her text included a phrase in English and we felt it was important to know that, there is a footnote to that effect; other editorial additions are between brackets or in italics. The maps show the most appropriate spelling for current linguistic standards of place-names.

Exact dating of Henry's photos is impossible – some are definitely from 1937/8, but there may be a few from 1946, perhaps even 1950, since format did not change as they were developed at UCD and not in a commercial lab. Nearly all of the photographs lack identification of any kind. When Henry began to prepare some of her boxes of materials to leave with the School of Archaeology at UCD in the late 1970s, she apparently tried to mark some locations on the backs of a few, but it is clear that she was not remembering all correctly. No names are given for any of the people appearing in her photographs. She was known to jealously guard her camera and tried to avoid appearing in photographs throughout her life. Based upon testimony of descendants and following descriptions in Henry's text, I have proposed identifications of those people and locations of which I feel most certain. Few suggestions are absolute, however, and anyone who can more surely identify any person or location is welcome to write to me at jtmarquardt@eiu.edu, so that any future editions may be corrected. All photographs are by Françoise Henry, unless otherwise indicated.

1937 journal[1]

French boats. Oh, the captain fixed a barometer for me that I'd brought from America and that wasn't set to the climate here. He took it all apart, piece by piece, and after that, it worked. If I'd known all the trouble that was involved, I'd never have asked him. One day I arrived, and there was the captain drinking his tea. And beside his cup was a sheet of paper, and he was writing, writing so fast you could hardly see it.

Pádr[aig][2] – Of course, you remember the day the French unloaded all that building wood they had brought, and they wrote their accounts in the sand with their fingers, and there was a mile of shore written on before they finished.

And they drink wine like we drink tea. That captain, he gave me two bottles of brandy and two of rum, ten shillings each, and it was good.

Slieve Mór,[3] like a big upturned boat. The waves iced with light. The rumbling, the dull blows of the waves breaking on the rocks – a green flash, and then an explosion of foam.

Night was falling. Greys and blacks, dull, confused. In the west, dazzling slashes of pale gold and silver – a brilliant world seen through shutter slats. The red eye of the lighthouse,[4] very far off, opening at regular intervals on its pyramid islet, like an irritating toy. Silver shimmers were freezing – silks spread out on the damp sand of the crescent shore, which was assailed by the ever-renewed procession of unfurling waves.

The swell of the rising breaker, which freezes for a second, hollow right the way along, stiff as a half-tube of green steel, only suddenly to collapse, first at one end, then more and more quickly along its whole length, in a dazzling cascade.

---

1 The first notebook, 20 by 16cm, is titled 'Fallmore/Avril 1937' on the cover. It is listed as FH/B8/273 (3) in the RIA archives. The first page contains a note: 'It's almost M. Dillon's Irish which is in the dictionary'. Myles Dillon (1900–72), philologist and specialist on Celtic studies, studied in France under the direction of Joseph Vendryes. He was at UCD with Françoise Henry until 1937, when he left to pursue his career in the US. Henry means that the people spoke an Irish very similar to that in his Gaelic dictionary.   2 Or Patrick.   3 Slievemore (Irish *Sliabh Mór*: 'Big Mountain'), the highest peak on Achill island. Altitude: 671m.   4 Blackrock Lighthouse, installed in 1864 on the islet 'Carraig Dubh', also known as 'An Tor' (the mound).

15 Men gathering kelp on to donkeys on the beach at Fallmore with outline of Slievemore, Achill, behind.

The old cemetery with its stones crudely fashioned into a cross, and eaten away by lichen at the heads of the graves. And the graves covered with big pebbles.[5] As the night became more indistinct, the two remnants of the old church walls, very black, stood out oddly against the glittering sadness of the sunset.

On the way back, one could make out the instability of the sea, faintly caressed by the remaining light – on it the dark masses of Achill, smothered by clouds, like a sleeper beneath an eiderdown.

৯ 10 April ৯

Sparkling day. Achill – the careened mass of Slievemore, then a long curve that bends down, hollows out and slowly climbs back up, then this land's end, as if someone had chopped the rock with great blows, and these amputated stumps of a vanished world stand as if to defy space and ocean. All this in a dark blue in which, as the light rises, there gradually appears a monstrous skeletal frame, so that the eye looks for the forms of a half-submerged dragon

5 These white 'pebbles' come from the shore and are quite large.

beneath this red hide that reveals itself little by little. All this looking out on the immense glittering of the sea and the low islets, which seem to float on it.

On the shore's edge, the black boats of the people of Inishkea, beached, their sharp prow standing out against the blue of the sea and the mountains.[6] The village of Inisht.,[7] cement houses all to the same design, along a new road – a little like a miners' garden city, behind which the backdrop of an epic had been accidentally rolled out.

Donkeys climb back up from the beach dripping with seaweed, their little noses as if bent down in the shadow of the gleaming mass of rubbery ribbons on top of them. Sand dunes behind them. In front of one of the houses, two men in blue jerseys spread out face down in the sun, and conversing. They make resounding comments on the weather, and smile broadly. Elsewhere, imperceptible movements of curtains, a shadow in the corner of a porch, a silhouette that tries to spy from the shadow of a gable, absorbed in it.

Went back down to the boats. A man is returning from the shore. While we are talking, there appear from who knows where – footsteps muffled by the sand – the two blue jerseys I saw just now. One of them wearing a sort of khaki cap, which was once perhaps a policeman's hat, but which has stretched into a Neapolitan cap,[8] quite young, red facial hair and a close haircut – what one can see of it – quick to smile, a lively glance. The first has that head hung a little in front of the shoulders, with a jutting jaw and a bristling red moustache, which is often found here. They are holding on to the sides of the boat, one beside the other. The island? Ah, it has its good and bad points. Land? Yes, there was certainly land on the island. And what's more you were very near the fish. Here, you're so much further away. Interesting, these men of Inishkea are the first in Ireland that I have ever seen put fishing ahead of everything. And yet, shaking his head, Red Moustache declares: The young people don't care for it, going out to sea.

---

6 Henry is describing Port Mór (Tóin na hUlltaí), the dock at Surgeview (formerly Nakil) and point of departure for the Inishkeas, which were situated directly opposite. Large boats went from Blacksod port. 7 Incomplete place-name, which Henry abbreviated as her writing reached the edge of the paper. It seems that she was referring to the new houses of the displaced islanders, who were settled on the mainland after the evacuation of the islands, as 'Inishkea', suggesting a sort of replacement settlement for the islands. They were given a house and 4–5 acres each on 400 acres between between Surgeview and Glosh. A 'new road' was built on the remains of the old track, leading from Port Mór (south coast) to Port Ghlais (Glosh), bordered by new houses with slate roofs. See Rita Nolan, *Within the Mullet* (Galway, 1998), p. 204. Henry's 'new road' is now called the 'Congo Road' by locals in reference to the first Congolese civil war (1960–4), which occurred at the same time that the road was rebuilt.   8 *bonnet napolitain*.

Was with Moira at a wake.[9] We leave by the road over the hill, chatting from time to time – it is clear that Moira does not get out much, everything is news to her.[10] Up above, a man runs out of the house with pink walls and joins us. Then another, further on. Then it's a big lad, black hair, long face, with darting eyes, and very frayed trousers, who lets himself slide off a little wall he had been sitting on, picks up his briar pipe and falls in behind us. We talk about so-and-so's health, and the weather, and some bits of news. Then tiredness gradually takes over, and we hardly speak anymore, until, after a prolonged silence, the man walking on my left cries out: Ah, but is no one going to speak at all? I don't like walking in silence like this! Everyone laughs. Then a tanned little woman, with short curls emerging from a beret pulled down tight into a ball, wearing a tweed coat she seems to have been fit into, as if she were made of wood. I speak Irish with difficulty.[11]

Desolate country. Sand dunes rising slightly on the left, flat greenish fields, and houses stuck here and there – mostly new houses, which seem to have been set down on the ground without being properly attached to it. A thin strip of very blue sea appears on the right at times, and beyond, dancing in the light, the low hills of Mayo.

We go into the kitchen. Rows of women in shawls, and men smoking pipes, silent, lined up on the benches, along the wall and in the middle of the room. Moira goes into the bedroom, kisses the dead woman on the forehead, and stays looking at her for a long time. Behind her, everyone in our group has knelt down. When, after kneeling in her turn, she gets back up, she takes two chairs and presses them against the window beside the corpse, for her, me and the girl in the tweed coat. A girl, in black and very elegant, approaches – the granddaughter who is a nurse in a London hospital. She and Moira speak for a moment about the deceased. Then Moira, with her youthful laugh, which she tries to stifle, tells the story of Annie,[12] who stayed until three o'clock in the morning making tea for the wake-goers, then finally, sent home exhausted by her aunt, notices a donkey. But she was in front of the house, and the donkey's owner was there, so she starts gently throwing stones at the donkey, till it was out of sight in the night. Then mounts it and heads off home like

---

9 'Moira' (Mary or Máire) Keane, wife of Stephan (Stephen) Keane. In their house, 'Sea View', in Fallmore, they kept a grocery shop and let out rooms.   10 In the original, the unconventional French '*Tout est nouvelle*'.   11 The French here reads '*parle*', which is ambiguous between first and third person, but first rather more likely as Henry was the least fluent of them all.   12 Annie Gaughan, a local girl, whose mother had died, raised by the Keanes. Throughout the text, Ann or Áine refers to Ann Cawley, while Annie is this younger girl.

that. They keep talking in a half-whisper, with occasional stifled laughs. To my left, Blue Tweed blows loudly and sniffs. Beside her the deceased, an ashen-faced old woman, rests on the bed, wrapped like a mummy in her brown habit with a scapular on her chest, and a panel of skirt material around her feet and hands, both wrapped in white gauze. All the holy pictures of the house have been taken down and surround her, two Christs looking to heaven, identical, a large apparition of the Virgin of L[ourdes?], and her feet are almost resting on a pope giving the blessing. From time to time, people come in, kneel. Old women in shawls are seated on two benches facing each other. One of them, her hand to her face, sniffs and rocks back and forth, asking herself perhaps why she is not keening. Some younger women, wearing fur-collared coats and Basque berets almost in a ball, with untidy hair, dreadfully ugly, a bony, big-nosed ugliness with irregular, protruding teeth, come in to join the group.

After an hour, M[oira] makes as if to leave, refuses some tea, refuses again, and finally goes to ask me if I would like some, to give herself an excuse to accept it.

We are brought into the third room. In the kitchen, a girl, from time to time, passes a plate filled with clay pipes. The silent men take one or put one back. I am sure that the women sitting with the deceased had asked for pipes, but the nurse played deaf. She congratulates herself that the wake has been so calm, with none of the customary disturbances.

In the third bedroom, two beds with multicoloured counterpanes. The coffin, its brass handles gleaming, leant on the wall and on one of the beds, and nearby a plateful of pipes.

৯ 11 April ৵

Still weather. Dark mountains set down on the sea. Clouds hanging from the sky like dust-covered drapery.

Burial (men bringing stones from the shore). Grave begun only when the hearse arrives. An ordinary cart – orange[13] – men walking (from the chapel three miles away),[14] women join from each house. Men all in navy blue woollens and caps. Stefan[15] in his light grey and very stiff home-spuns. During the burial, a boat breaks off from the quay down below, and a russet sail slowly raises its triangle in the grey air.

---

13 Carts were all painted a red-orange in that area at the time. 14 Tiraun chapel ['Tír Áine', Anne's land]. 15 Stephan (Stephen) Keane, husband of Mary.

16 One loaded donkey returning from the beach; one heading down for another load.

Annie tries to convince some boys here and there to take us. Not much enthusiasm – too late, and the currachs haven't been tarred, it would be like wading in the sea, or indeed this lot don't have a currach.[16] When we were about to give up, three big lads come running up – the three Pádraigs whom M[oira] has convinced, I know not by what arguments, and who are overflowing, bursting with spirit.[17] A currach? Oh, they don't have one. But for sure the old king of Inishkea will lend them one. And they send Annie across the sands to one of the houses in the mining village,[18] and go down to the quay with me. They examine a few black hulls, holed and patched up, touch them, pinch them, strike them, as with an animal at market. Philip's one there? No, maybe this one? Finally, Annie comes back with a boy in a white

16 A *currach*, also spelled *curragh*, was the standard small sea craft of the islands made of a wood frame with stretched canvas. There were two styles, that of Achill and the one used by the people of the Inishkeas, which was narrower, with a higher prow and no keel.   17 From the photograph with the swan, we know that at least two of these boys were not named Pádraig (Patrick), but are John and Dominic Lavelle. They may have been teasing Henry that all boys in Ireland are named 'Paddy' or she may have simply called them that mistakenly.   18 There was a village built by the company who constructed the lighthouse at Blacksod in the 1860s for workers in the quarry from which good quality granite (white, dark red and pale yellow) was shipped all over Europe. It was called Baile an Chladaigh and is now gone. It was separate from the 'new town' for the islanders. Situated at the southern tip of the peninsula, a small railway led from the 'mining village' to Blacksod port, from where the granite was exported. See Nolan, *Within the Mullet*, pp 101–3.

17 Men carrying a currach, seen from front.

jersey. The currach is lifted up, makes its way like a beetle and sits very carefully in the water. The three P[ádraigs] row like devils. It is raining over there behind Slievemore and something tells me the wind will pick up, but they pay no heed to it. They strike the water with sharp strokes of their narrow little oars, and the several peaks at the end of Achill spread out one after the other, in a hard, massive russet-blue. The foamless sea swells and sinks, and the three P[ádraigs] row, row and announce that they are headed for America, and joke with Annie, and ask her to sing. The rain hides the jagged heights of Croaghaun,[19] but we are going towards clear sky, and the sea is all spangled with silver like grey shadows on milk.[20]

19 Croaghaun ['Cruachán'], 668m, second peak of Achill. In the original, the author consistently writes 'Clochaun', a form which we have corrected to avoid confusion.   20 In the manuscript, the facing page contains the following: 'Cormorants like black [?] sometimes flying very low over the sea like a [?] seized by vertigo'.

18 Men carrying a currach, seen from behind.

Arriving near the island,[21] we meet the boat, which has brought some livestock there. The men wave to us. The boat passes us, and stands, very black, against a tragic landscape where the rain sluices down over great mountainous slabs.[22] The island is low-lying, with sandy dunes opposite the mainland, and a village tucked away, encircling a little bay. Approaching, one sees that the houses, most of them still standing, have holes in their roofs and gaping doors. The first is full of lobster pots. From the second emerge, looking a little dazed, a man and a woman carrying a baby. All around is only desolation, ducks waddling among ruins. We climb up to the *teampull* Colum Cille,[23] on the hill. My crew searches with care and some curiosity for the 'stone with a cross' that I hoped to find there. In vain. We go back down to the village, the P[ádraigs] making as if to knock on closed doors, asking the crumbling walls for a cup of tea, one asking if I wouldn't like to settle down with him there. Finally, life again: an inhabited house, into which we go. An old woman, her face stunningly pink and smiling, two girls with their long hair hanging down, four small children. They sit us down, Annie and me, to have tea.

---

21 This is Inishkea North.　**22** Namely, the jagged heights of Croaghaun.　**23** The chapel of St Columba, or Colum Cille, an Irish missionary and founder of the monastery at Iona (Scotland).

19 Church of St Colum Cille on Inishkea North, called the 'oratory' and 'teampull' by Henry (photograph by Janet Marquardt, June 2011).

The man comes in, maybe 50 years old, a face covered in red hair, but one sees only his very blue eyes, an intense, opaque blue. I say to him: *Is cosm[h]ail go b[h]fuil an áit sin uaigneac[h] anois?* ['That place must be lonely now?'] To which, his gaze lost in the distance, he responds: *Tá sé uaigneac[h], ach tá sé suai[bh]n[e]ach freisin* ['It's lonely, but it's peaceful too'], and with acrobatic efforts to speak English he explains to me that in summer it is full of birds. And since I ask: sea birds? He shakes his head, probably not understanding very well, and responds: Ah, we don't really know, I don't know the species, all sorts of birds. Then, excusing himself with a circular gesture: It's all topsy turvy here, five years ago we thought we'd be leaving soon, and we're still here. Just then, the crew, who stayed outside with the two boys, call me loudly: they are holding a wild swan by the wings and want me to photograph it. A light brown swan, which hurt itself and got caught in the little lake to the north of the island. It protests a little and makes as if to hiss, but when I bring my hand near, it just dips its head a little, and lets me stroke its down as soft as fur. When I go back into the house, the woman is sitting on a low stool, her knees up, while the four small children squat in a semi-circle beside her around the fire, showing only the tousled hair on their necks, and the curious profile of one of the girls.

20 Two boys posing with the wounded swan on Inishkea North. They have been identified as John and Dominic Lavelle (see p. 35, n. 17).

We go down to the shore with the eldest of the girls. She seems a little vacant and hangs her head slightly forward like most of the islanders, but her face is made stunning by her huge blue eyes surrounded by black lashes, whose looks fall on you all at once. We go down towards my stone slab (stele), which is right down on the sands, and while I photograph it, I hear her and Annie talking: Would you prefer the village on the mainland or this one? Oh, this one, of course! This is said in a resigned tone, but as an obvious truth. We go as far as the cemetery, a little enclosed patch of dry stones with a view of the sands on one side, on the other the sea, which foams a few paces away. All the graves there are laid with white stones, and marked by a branch stuck in the earth, a forest of silvery stumps, which stands, slender, spindly, before the dark and shifting sea.

As we return,[24] the sea is unclear like a cloudy sky. To the west, a curtain seems to be rising slowly over undefined spaces of brightness. The two islands are only thin lines embossed on the surface of the waves. Over the mountains, which are being reborn after the rain, run shivers of gold and purple. When we climb back, all five of us, towards the village,[25] a ray of the setting sun shoots

24 To the mainland. 25 Fallmore.

21 Stephan Keane outside 'Seaview House', where Henry stayed in 1937.

out at last and over the periwinkle-blue sea, the sea that seems not to notice, it sets Slievemore aflame, paints it suddenly in hues of burning embers, of glowing embers striped with black shadows.

After supper, the three P[ádraig]s appear one after the other. One of them takes an accordion from a corner and starts to play. St[ephan] appears, still in his stiff home-spuns, and is put upon to take his fiddle out of its case, which he does with obvious pleasure and all kinds of excuses. While he is playing, the door opens and St[ephen] Lavelle appears, hairy and dark, his cap without deco[ration?][26] behind, over a stiff brush of hair, looking wary. The P[ádraig]s nudge him: Dance St[ephen], go on, dance! I thought they were joking. But St[ephen], after a few grunts, gets up, turning his back to us, his legs set a little apart, his body hunched up, and listens, rocking back and forth. Then, still showing us only his bouncing behind, and his big, waving blue smock, he starts to dance, displaying obvious knowledge and the instincts of a performing bear.

Sort of fog. Came back from Blacksod by the top of the hill. A slight impression of walking while looking down: the hill plunges everywhere into a blue-tinted imponderable where there floats, half-way down, the golden line of faraway shores. A woman drying turf on a low wall right up on the hill. Bad turf, practically earth.[27] Arrived in the mining village. From behind the downy

26 Illegible word, again running off edge of page, seems to begin '*déco*'.   27 The colour of this turf gave Blacksod its name.

clouds enveloping it, the sun explores with long orangey looks, the grey space. It reveals with coppery strokes the shimmering water there, and below, between two streaks of gold, the embossed silhouette of Inishkea.

Miss Cronin.[28] Story of the *Naomhóg*.[29]

The N[aomhóg] was a miraculous statue which was br[ought] to Inishk[ea] by one of the early Ir[ish] saints. It is supposed that it came from Italy as it was called the Bambino also. An Ir[ish] s[ain]t named Gé went to live on the island. It is thought she brought the statue with her. And for a long time it was kept in the church of Col[umcille] on the north island. When the Danes were plundering the Ir[ish] churches they made several attempts to come ashore on In[ishkea] but never succeeded. The people kept a sharp look out for them and whenever they were seen approaching, the S[ain]t gathered the people before the statue and said certain prayers. After these prayers were said, the sea became very angry and no boat was able to land. As soon as the Danish boats sailed away, the S[ain]t and the people recited other prayers before the stat[ue] and the waves fell and became calm again. This practice continued after the S[ain]t's death and the stat[ue] still retained its miraculous power. When the old church fell, the statue was taken in to the best house[30] on the island and a special niche was made for it in the wall. One time some sea-rob[b]ers came ashore unknown to the people and plundered the island. They burned all the houses on the island but could not succeed in setting fire to the one in which the N[aomhóg] was kept. The capt[ain] thought this very strange, so he made inquiries to find out the cause. When he was told of the N[aomhóg] and underst[ood] that it was its power that had prevented him from landing on the island many times before, he seized it and smashed[31] it on the rocks. When the N[aomhóg] was removed from the house, he had no trouble in

28 Mary K. Cronin, schoolteacher in Aughleam. As she explains in a letter of 25 January 1935, addressed to Adolf Mahr, director of the NMI, after the evacuation of the Inishkeas, most of the islanders' children joined her school, where she encouraged them to take an interest in their heritage: 'there are two islands – the north and the south. The former is the more interesting from an archaeological point of view. Up to a short time ago, there were sixty families living on the islands. These migrated lately to the mainland and the children now come to school to me. It is from these little ones I got the information about the island that I sent you' (Archives, NMI, ref. 1935:28.33). Furthermore, on 20 January 1935, Mary Cronin sent a description of the *Naomhóg* to the museum, which is very close to that reproduced by Françoise Henry.   29 Henry's record of the legend as told to her by Miss Cronin is contained in the second small, 11.5 by 8cm, black notebook written in English and in pencil, marked in black ink on the cover 'Fallmore/Avril 1937' and in red 'Naomhóg' and 'Naimhog'. It is listed as [FH/B8/273 (1) (i)] in the RIA archives and inserted here for continuity of the narrative.   30 In the original, the word 'statue' was replaced by 'house'.   31 In the original, the words 'many times' were replaced by 'smashed'.

setting it on fire. Next day the people gathered the pieces of the statue and bound them together with cord. From that time out, they dressed it in a new flan[n]el coat every year so that no one might know it was broken. It still had the same power, but the people never used it unless somebody on the island was very ill and required a priest in time of storm. They had recourse to it then to calm the waters.

One time, a barrel of petrol was washed ashore on the island. The people did not know it was inflammable and divided it in the house in wh[ich] the N[aomhóg] was kept. A woman held a candle close to the barrel to give | them light and the house went on fire. The woman and the men were badly burnt, also the whole kitchen, but the flames never touched the room in which the N[aomhóg] was kept. At the time of the Famine, some prosel[ytizers] came from Achill to try to induce the people to give up their relig[ion]. They were very friendly tow[ards] the people and gave sweets to the children and promised to return in a month's time with clothes and food. They asked many quest[ions] about the Nao[mhóg] and, as they were so kind and friendly, the people answered them freely. Soon after they returned to A[chill], a letter from one of them (Nash or Nangle) app[eared] in the *Ir[ish] Times* saying that there were people on the is[land] of In[ishkea] calling themselves Cath[olic] who were in reality pagans, as they kept a false god called the N[aomhóg], which they worshipped. The parish priest of Kilmore, Fr Patr[ick] O'Rahilly,[32] saw the letter and was very angry with the In[ishkea] people. As it was drawing near the time for the Easter stations, he went into In[ishkea] and reprim[anded] the people severely. He ordered them to give him the statue and then he cast it into the sea. The priest did not know it was a Christ[ian] statue and really bel[ieved] they were using it as a charm or idol. Betw[een] the years 1900 and 1910, Canon O'R – came to the parish. He took a gr[eat] int[erest] in antiqu[ities]. He heard of the N[aomhóg] and did his best to find out what it was. It was he that found it was of Chr[istian] origin and that it was called the Bambino, when it first came to the country. He paid a visit to the island and inquired if there was anyone there who could ident[ify] the statue. Two old men told him they would know it if they saw it. Then he sent the young boys of the island to the place where Fr O'R[ahilly] was supposed to have thrown the statue. They found a red slab which the old men ident[ified] as the lower portion of the statue. Canon O'R – took this away with him but it

---

32 One finds the following variants of the family name of this priest: 'O'Reilly' and 'Reilly'. See T.H. White, *The Godstone and the Blackymor* (London, 1959), p. 114; Brian Dornan, *Mayo's lost islands: the Inishkeas* (Dublin, 2000), pp 249–50.

is not known what he did with it. The Inishk[ea] people say that the sea is always calm at the spot where the N[aomhóg] was thrown and that boats and c[attle] can come ash[ore]. There are rough days when it is imposs[ible] to come ashore on any other place on the island.

Made of terra cotta about a foot long.[33]

[Return to pick up the narrative in the first notebook FH/B8/273 (3)]
Came back from Miss Cronin's house at night. The clear sea can be faintly made out beneath the new moon with its ring trembling in the sky. One hears it above all, filling the space, bringing it to life like the presence of an animal in an absent cowshed. This faraway noise which is like a vital pulse, and, rising and falling, swelling and subsiding, like breath lifting up a chest, its respiration on the shores.

Down through Glosh. Lights in all the windows. Silhouettes that emerge suddenly from the night, bid you an *oíche mhaith* ['good night'] as they pass, and whom one hears murmuring something (*franncach*) ['Frenchwoman'].

❧ 14 April ❧

Fog. The sea has no bounds. Went down to the shore. Two women gathering seaweed with forks. The younger wearing a black beret pulled down over her scattered locks, prodigiously ugly, a dull ugliness, except when a smile of goodwill crinkles her round face. The other, Sarah Lavelle, tall, a bit gangly, with grey hair tangled beneath a black linen scarf, a bony, mobile face, of stunning freshness, with shining blue eyes and a mouth so expressive that she seems to speak before uttering a word. Reflections on the weather, and then Sarah lets it be known that she would like very much to have her picture taken. But she is seized by an attack of vanity as soon as I point my camera at her. She throws down her fork and, with great movements of her arms and hips, looks for the strings of her homespun apron. Wait a minute till I make myself look nice! Apparently she is the sister of the blue-eyed man on the island.[34]

33 On the inside back cover of this notebook: 'Inishkea North. Granite, about 1.80 high'. Some loose leaves have drawn lines showing horizontal dimensions '0.40 et 0.32' as well as vertical '0.70'. There are also jotted notes: *nullement du varech* [no seaweed] and 'Miss Lavelle W[illia]m/Glosh/Belmullet'.
34 According to Tom Reilly, grandson of Pat Reilly, Sarah Lavelle was the sister of Pat 'Cheit' Lavelle. Although she will later claim to be unmarried in speaking with Henry (see pp 45–6, n. 36), the French text here clearly indicates that Henry is not referring to Sarah's brother when she says she was married on the island and stays there.

22 Sarah Lavelle and Biddy Keane Stephan raking kelp on Fallmore beach.

Was born in Australia. Got married on the island last year. Has hardly left it since ... Do you prefer being on the island or here? Oh, here, we can go to Mass. – There was no Mass on the island? – The other interjects: No, but the mistress said the Rosary in the school every Sunday; I liked that a lot too.

Curious, here it is the old who like the new houses, and the younger people who regret them.

The sea speaks loudly on the sand behind us. The tide rises, and all of a sudden my feet are in the water. The two of them burst out laughing. There is not a breath of wind and yet, from those unreal depths where it vanishes, the sea slams with all its force against the sand, against the rocks. Long breakers on the shore, which roll in with crunching and foaming, as if the sand were being gnawed to exhaustion. Explosions on the rocks, dull, violent, a force coming from one knows not where, that seems the herald of distant dramas.

In the afternoon, gleams of light run about, the islands seem to be born out of the sea. Achill, strip by strip, reveals itself, pale and brushed by a sun come from who knows where.

In the night, the noise of the sea, sometimes like a train pounding the silence, one of those express trains that tear up the sleeping countryside with sparks. Then the shouts of a crowd, a crowd cheering or booing – who knows – there, behind that bend in the street, and its passion alone reaches you – ooh, oh,

23 Sarah Lavelle, 'tall, a bit gangly, with grey hair tangled beneath a black linen scarf, a bony, mobile face, of stunning freshness, with shining blue eyes and a mouth so expressive that she seems to speak before uttering a word'.

ah, ooh-oo-oo-oh, and who knows whether it is calling for death or frenzied with joy. Then over this manifold noise the dull blows, pow, wham, ah! – which at times shake the rocks, followed by a collapsing cascade.

On the mother-of-pearl sea, the islets are each like a cake in its crinkled paper, so permanent seems their crown of foam.

❧ 15 April ❧

Rain. My going down through Glosh arouses some curiosity. People hastily cross the road so that they can make some remark to me, women stand unabashed in the doorways. Sarah appears suddenly from the corner of a low wall, a *báinín* tied around her waist, a scarf on her shoulders, a faded pink coat serving as a shawl on her head. I give voice to my idea of spending a few days on the island next month. Oh, the simplest thing is for you to get married and settle down there. Hearing my protestations, she objects: Ah, but all the same it would be nice to have children – me, I never got married [until now], and look at the people you're living with, who don't have any children.[35] What a pity!

35 This is a reference to the Keanes, who reared Annie Gaughan but had no children of their own. If the speaker is Sarah Lavelle, however, Henry has recorded her statement slightly in error as she just stated on 14 April that Sarah had married on the island the previous year. She was older than usual, however, and

I try out my idea on Annie that evening. Exactly the same reaction as Julia would have: Oh yes, of course, that could be arranged, and (with glowing eyes) I'd go with you! Like Julia, for whom it was a marvellous adventure to go with me to Lettercallow[36] in the boat, or Barbara,[37] who had arranged everything despite her father for me to go with Padraig Mhikil. This taste for adventure that possesses all of them.

The O'Rahillys [O'Reillys], those whom we saw first, did not have land in Glosh, married and went to the island.[38] They have been there for two years. One baby, another on the way. Looks like they'll stay. The others are leaving this summer.

❧ 17 April ❧

The youngest of the Paidr[aig]s, tousled, putting on a 'bold' air to joke with me: Is it for me you're making a jumper? – For you, of course, and wait and see how the *cailíní* ['girls'] will make fun of you! – Ah, the divil! (glance at the clock) Will it be finished for tomorrow? – Finished for tomorrow? Oh yes, I'm going to knit all night for you! – Henri [Harry] comes in, his face that of an old Moor [?],[39] with yellow teeth past his thick moustache, a face which one would say had been forcibly lengthened, and had remained forever stunned at the procedure. Stephan talks about the places where he has worked in England. Have you been to Newcastle? – Yes. – And Leith? – Yes, I went from there to Orkney and Shetl[and]. You saw the island where there are gulls everywhere? I met a captain who had been there and he said that it was covered in gulls. – Yes. And then there are seals too, hundreds of seals. – Hundreds! – P[ádraig] interjects: There are seals here too. You'll see some at Devilaun[40] tomorrow when I bring you there (punctuated with a shake of the head: 'See the entertainment I'm going to give you!') – Do they kill seals around here? – St[ephan]: There are people who kill them for the skin ... Me: I wouldn't like to kill a seal. They look too human. – H[arry]: You are right, the seals were men once, just like the swans. – M[e]: The swans? – St[ephan]: The

---

may have been making reference to that, thinking it was too late for her to have children. In fact, she would later have one daughter. We have thus added 'until now' to the quote.   **36** In Connemara. **37** Neither Julia nor Barbara can be identified.   **38** This is again referring to Inishkea North.   **39** Illegible French, looking like 'Mohr' and suggesting the word 'Maure'. Harry was Stephan Keane's brother, said to be a great authority on local folklore.   **40** Usual spelling 'Duvillaun' ['Dubh Oileán': 'black island']. The author also writes 'Dovelaun' and 'Develaun', but these have been standardized here. The name refers to an island near the Inishkeas, Duvillaun [Mór] – there is also Duvillaun Beg.

children of Lir,[41] you know, who were turned into swans ... P[ádraig] (to me): Like the swan we showed you at Inishkea on Sunday, you know. – Máire: A swan? – P[ádraig]: Yes, a young swan that had hurt himself. There are three of them in the lake. Oh, they'll let that one go when he's cured. And he's not wild. She (pointing to me) put her hand on his head and he didn't move. – Máire, dreaming, looks into the fire – Me: But seals are much more like people. – H[arry]: Ah, of course. – Máire (who has never seen a seal): Like people? – H[arry]: Yes, they have hands with proper nails, and faces like you and me. – Me: That's strange. H[arry]: Why is it strange? Don't you know that everything that exists on land exists in the sea too? – Me: Yes, I've heard that said (Mac Dara on Inishmaan), and that there are horses in the sea ... – H[arry]: Horses? – Yes, probably, but mermaids[42] in any case. – Me: Mermaids? – H[arry] and P[ádraig] (in chorus): Yes. – M[e]: You've seen one? – H[arry] shakes his head: Better not to. – Máire: If you see one, you don't live out the year. – Me (to H[arry]): Is that true? – H[arry]: Ah, it depends: if she comes towards you, you won't die, but if you see her go off, then you will surely die. There's a lad down below the village who saw one, but she was coming towards him, so he didn't die. – P[ádraig]: And then there's a man who walks in the sea with a lantern in his hand. – Me: In the sea? – P[ádraig]: Yes, when the weather is bad. If not, he walks on the shore. H[arry]: Ah, all the things you see on the sea. One day when people were fishing in a currach, they saw a boat and there was one who knew, and who said to the others: That there is a boat that you only see when the weather is going to be bad, it's the boat of rain and gales (*b[áisteach] agus gála*). We need to go back. And the others just laughed. But he was right ... – P[ádraig]: And then there's a dog in the sea.[43] –M[e]: A

---

41 According to the legend, the children of Lir (Finola and her brothers Aedh, Conn and Fiachra) had a cruel stepmother, their aunt, who was jealous of their love for her sister, Eve, their dead mother. She transformed them into swans but they kept their human nature and the power of speech and music. The spell was meant to last until a prince from the north married a princess from the south and the couple heard church bells of the new Christian faith. There are varying stories about which islands off the northwest coast of Ireland (near the Inishkeas) they spent time – usually counted in sets of 300 years. One version has them finally on Inishglora Island, where St Kemoc changed them back into humans. Another has the swans end up on Bird Lake in Clare Island and they are taken in by St Mohévog, who took them to his dwelling to attend Mass. Here, it is only when some people tried to capture them that their plumage fell away. In all versions, they were left as elderly people who took Christian baptism before their death.   42 The '*maighdean mara*' is very present in the local folklore, as are otherworldly beliefs about seals. Examples of some regional mermaid tales can be found in Angela Bourke, 'Economic necessity and escapist fantasy in Éamon A Búrc's sea-stories' and stories about seals in Bairbre Ní Fhloinn, 'Tadhg, Donncha and some of their relations: seals in Irish oral tradition' both in P. Lysaght, S. Ó Catháin and D. Ó hÓgáin (eds), *Islanders and water-dwellers* (Dublin, 1999), pp 19–35.   43 The Irish for 'otter' is *madra uisce*, literally 'water dog'.

dog? – P[ádraig]: Yes, oh really he's no bigger than a cat, and he comes onto the shore to eat the fish he catches. They make collars out of him for coats, you know (otter).

❧ 16 April [*sic*] ❧

Mikil Phat, and his cousin, Martin Lavelle came to say goodbye. We were in the kitchen when they burst in, like big lanky dogs, and flopping onto the bench, declared: We're leaving today. Stephan, rather pompously, turned to me: They are leaving for Glasgow, because there is no work here for them, you understand. The two lads nodded their heads. They will take a lorry to Belmullet. And then the day after to Ballina, and then another to Sligo, and then from there to Derry, to get the boat. Mikil, the 'captain' of the crew, affects gaiety and an offhand air. He has a stubborn and fearless face, tanned by the sun, half-childish when he smiles, with very bright eyes, circled by black lashes, eyes that look so far ahead that nothing close by must satisfy them, and a greedy mouth, with a swollen lower lip. The face of a lad who would play every mean trick, or show every kind of devotion. The other's face is sheep-like and calm.

After exchanging a few remarks rather loudly, to hide their nerves, they unfold from their places on the bench and swing towards the door. But Máire, who has slipped into the shop, grabs Martin's hand as he passes and slips something into it. M[artin] tries to protest. Mikil watches, a little sulkily. Yes, yes, Máire insists, take it, and she forces a pound note into the boy's fingers. Turning to Mikil: It's for both of you, of course. You'll be together on the boat. You'll need it. When they have gone, she turns to me, and becomes voluble: You understand, I couldn't give it to Mikil, he can't keep hold of money. As soon he has a shilling he goes off to spend it in the pub in Blacksod.

That evening, squeezed into a *báinín* smock, like the peasants' smocks back home, Patrick Lavelle, Martin's father, comes in.[44] He sits down on the bench, and leaning over to Stephan, who is finishing his tea most solemnly, very 'head of the household', at the top of the table: You weren't at the fair? – No, the cow fell sick just the day before the fair. – Oh dear! then you won't be able to sell her before she has her four teeth? No (the end of St[ephan]'s nose moves back and forth). – What a shame, it's not worth raising her if you have to pay

---

44 Again, Henry may have made an error. Mikil Phat's nickname means that his father's name is Patrick and he is the one whom Máire suggests Patrick Lavelle will miss.

24 View of Slievemore 'hardly distinct' above a 'black sea' with 'clouds piled up'.

the tax when you sell her. – St[ephan] (very gloomy): But it's not worth it ... – A silence. – Patr[ick]: M[ikil Phat] came to see you? – St[ephan]: Yes. The two of them went off in the lorry. – Máire: You're going to miss him, Pádrik! – St[ephan] (interrupting): Oh, he'll get a good job in Glasgow! – Patr[ick]: Yes, I think so ... It's unfortunate all the same, this cow ... And she's no better? St[ephan] (very gloomy): No better, no better at all. – P[atrick]: Ah, I always say, better to raise pigs. With pigs, it's a sure business. You give them bran, you take good care of them, and so forth. The conversation becomes more and more technical. P[atrick] turns his head slightly. A beam of firelight plays on his face and makes some wet patches gleam at the corners of his eyes. – Better to raise pigs, believe me, with that, you're sure of your money ...

Was on the dunes. North wind that whipped the sea and the sand. Clouds of sand which made the face burn and eyes swell. The sea just now sparkling like molten glass in the sun with profusions of foam, an effervescence of snow. Then racing gusts of wind, a dark cloud rising from the horizon, trailing a curtain of rain behind. And the waves suddenly calm down, fray in the wind, fly off in panic-stricken manes. The heights of Croaghaun float in the sky, a jagged, unreal outline above this back-and-forth gallop.

Late on the shore. Slievemore hardly distinct, faintly mauve and pink and golden through a storm cloud struck by sunlight. The sea was black, breaking,

25 View of Duvillaun from Surgeview (photograph by Janet Marquardt, May 2011).

and blown back on itself by the wind. From the crest of a semi-circular wave ready to break on the sand, it whipped up suddenly a sort of ramp of white, blinding flames, so that the livid fire spread the length of the rocks. Then a collapse – the wave, escaping this disintegration, broke like snow falling from a roof. All the way to the horizon the clouds piled up, and the rocks burned white.

Blue sea, beneath the pale sky, every sort of blue rolled together into a delirious azure, and nonchalantly hemmed by a little white at the edge of the sands.

❧ 18 April ❧

With Tomás and Pádraig and Máire at Duvillaun.[45] Disembarked among the rocks. We haul up the currach, scratching it extensively on the rocks bristling with small mussels. (Currachs lined with thin planks. When there's no tar, with what do you waterproof the currachs? Even leather becomes damp after a while.) It remains there, its black beak standing out against the blue sea.

---

45 Cawley siblings from Fallmore and neighbours of Stephan and Máire Keane. They owned the *currach*.

26 Landing a currach on Duvillaun.

The island is quite high, covered with stunted heather. The remains of a road rising towards some ruined houses at the very top of the hill. From the summit of the hillock, set in blue, the cliffs of Croaghaun, russet and sparkling a little. Foam so white, so blinding on the rocks, at the bottom of the slope. Two more hills rise up. A little world, which, due to the presence of the great cliffs nearby, has an air of being sheltered, protected. A self-sufficient world, before bare immensities, where nothing stifles the spirit. With unexpected moments of softness, too – this pond at the edge of which a donkey and her foal were grazing, so humbly hairy, rough, cottony. The big stone slab standing at the highest point, gilded with sunlight, displaying like a great page its perfectly harmonious lines that are so little bound to reality. The serene beauty released by this primitive art.

P[ádraig] had set fire to the heather. The huge plume of smoke covered the curves of Slievemore with its curls.

On some rocks there burst out of the water, cormorants, two gannets and a few gulls.

[Third notebook][46]

iv. Rí Span. Naev. Derv. ['Four Spanish kings. St Deirbhile'[47]]

Agus sancta vita ['And holy life']

Two knees make holes in stone at the summit of the hill.[48]

Four Spanish kings came to Ireland.[49]

Seven years to come from Spain.

They were lost and could not find their way.

They made a cross with their hands. Then arrive in Ireland. Co. Antrim. O'Connor, O'Brien, O'Neil, O'Donnel. The time you would be rich you take the O'. But no other people with O'. But O' with every name now.

She came here. *Áit uaigneach, hanik she ansear* [*Áit uaigneach. Tháinig sí ionsair*: 'Lonely place, she came here'].[50]

Tiachín beag san chapeal a she corrig [*Teachín beag san séipéal i sé charraig*: 'Little dwelling in the chapel of the six rocks']. She came because this was the biggest place in Mayo with saints and she came to be with them.

Tarmon, a word which is neither English nor Irish, but Latin.[51]

The place where she was buried there is a stone with a cross on it and a lamb. And the grass never grows on it.

She had a Lamb of God with her. She died. The Lamb left, went down towards the shore, and leapt over to a little island near Dev[illaun].[52] It was never seen again.

Made the well so that the people could come to holy services. Never dries up.

---

46 The third notebook is like the first, 20 by 16cm. It is also untitled. It is listed as FH/B8/273 (2) in the RIA archives.   47 St Deirbhile, who according to the folk tradition lived on the island at the same time as St Gé. See also the sketch of 'Teampull Deirbhile' by Françoise Henry (IVRLA, FHC, Stones/Sites/Notes relating to the excavations at Inishkea County Mayo FHA, image 260).   48 To the west of the grave of St Deirbhile are found some stones, called 'Glúine an Asail' (the donkey's knees), supposed to mark the prints of the knees of the donkey which rested there after bringing the saint to her destination.   49 Allusion to the supposed Spanish origin of the native Irish (the 'Gaeil'), who, according to a version of the *Lebor Gabála Érenn*, descend from Mil Easpáinne (Miles, a Spanish warrior), following an invasion of Ireland led by his sons – Ir, Eibhear and Eireamhón. In the following lines, the reference to the O'Connor, O'Brien, O'Neil and O'Donne[l]l families seems to take up the reference again, even if the source's English seems imperfect.   50 St Deirbhile is supposed to have been so beautiful that she plucked out her eyes so as not to attract men's attentions, in particular those of a man who was madly in love with her.   51 'Tearmann' [Old Irish *termon*, retreat], a word which is perfectly valid in Irish, deriving from the Latin *terminus*. Termon, a granite outcrop 103 metres high, is the highest point of the Mullet Peninsula.   52 This allusion to the 'lamb of God' may have inspired the name of the tiny island that is found between the coast of Fallmore and Duvillaun called Leamareha or *Léim an Reithe* [Ram's Leap]. The channel, which separates the island from the continent, is called *Léim siar* [Westward Leap].

1 (*previous page*) Early Medieval stone slab on the Bailey Mór, Inishkea North
(photograph by Janet Marquardt, June 2011).

2 (*top*) Large stone slab standing to the east of the Bailey Mór on Inishkea North,
see also fig. 9 (photograph by Derek Gordon, April 2007).

3 (*bottom*) View down into cove, showing danger which worried Ann
(photograph by Janet Marquardt, June 2011).

4 (*top*) Weathered cross at the cemetery on Inishkea North looking east toward Blacksod Bay. In the far left background, one can make out the tower at Glosh on the mainland (see colour pl. 9) (photograph by Derek Gordon, April 2007).

5 (*bottom*) View of Slievemore, Achill, from Fallmore (photograph by Janet Marquardt, May 2011).

6 (*left*) 'French' lobster pot, example kept in Heritage Centre at Aughleam on the Mullet Peninsula (photograph by Janet Marquardt, May 2011).

7 (*below*) Achill heather lobster pot, example hanging in Heritage Centre at Aughleam on the Mullet Peninsula (photograph by Janet Marquardt, May 2011).

8 (*top*) Remains of dock at Port Mór (Surgeview) with new slip in foreground
(photograph by Janet Marquardt, May 2011).

9 (*bottom*) Napoleonic signal tower at Glosh, from where Henry imagined one
might see her candlelight in the little house on Inishkea North
(photograph by Janet Marquardt, May 2011).

10 (*top*) View to the south on Inishkea North along former village street showing eroded houses (photograph by Rick Hill, April 2007).

11 (*bottom*) View of remaining walls of lower village houses on Inishkea North (photograph by Janet Marquardt, June 2011).

12 (*top*) The bay at Inishkea North, showing two of the 'porteens' or small beaches and taken from 'Port Tragh' (port of the beach) (photograph by Janet Marquardt, June 2011).

13 (*bottom*) 'Almost all the flowers grow level with the ground, with tiny stalks' (see p. 117) (photograph by Janet Marquardt, June 2011).

14 (*next page*) St Deirbhile's Well at Fallmore (photograph by Janet Marquardt, May 2011).

27 Ram's Leap island seen from Fallmore cemetery (photograph by Alice Cherry, May 2011).

410[53]

That is how St Paul gained the whole world.[54] He and St Peter spoke and – .
Both feet [*4 illegible words: un na fla em*] [*Chun na bhflaitheas*: 'Towards
heaven'] *Solus en un boher* [*Solas chun an bhóthair*: 'Light for the road'].[55]

Inisglora. – *Broher Breanach ag banant Inis[h]glora agus vi van rive agus
dier shi ge pos shi é agus* [Four illegible words: '*apu palin cha' nu*] *agus hánig
shé. Ni she er slias san cloch agus d'acli liac agus – agus s'é un brá br.* [1 illegible
word: *nugl.*] [*Bráthair Bréanainn ag baint Inis[h]glora, agus bhí [an] bhean
roimhe agus deir sí go bpósfadh sí é [...] agus tháinig sé. Nígh sé an tslis san chloch
agus d'aclaigh liag agus – agus is é an bráth[air] Br[éanainn]*: ['Brother Brendan
reaching Inisglora, and there was a woman who met him and said she would
marry him [...] and he came. He washed the beater in the stone and made the
monument move and – and it is Brother Brendan'.]

53 We assume this is the date 410CE, which she is assigning to the legend.   54 Perhaps referring to Christ's
question: 'What shall it profit a man if he gains the entire world yet loses his soul?' (Mk 8:36).   55 St
Paul was converted when a great light from the sky caused him to fall off his horse on the road to Damascus
and he heard the Lord's voice asking him why he was so cruel to the Christians. See Acts 9:3–7.

1 5 August circuit of the well.

3 times all around kneeling. 3 times walking. 3 Decades of the Rosary. 7 Paters, 7 Aves and *Credo na n-Aspal* [the Apostles' Creed]. Drink the water 3 times. For whatever sickness. Never thirsty again after having drunk the water of the well.

Niev. Kiérol ar Develaun.[56] Lives in Dev[elaun]. For a while.
St Brendan to Inishglora after having been to America and stays until his death.[57]

Left from Limerick in a *corrochín beag* ['little currach']. Horse skin on the currach.

Comes back from America to Limerick and from there to Inishglora,[58] *tsi na deenie beanuig balach seo* [*tchí na daoine beannaithe* [*an*] *bealach seo*: 'blessed people see thus'].

Weather was bad when he arrived *agus* ['and'] old people say: *Rihe glas na fear Brenann* [*Reithe glas na fearthainne*: 'The grey ram of the rain'].

He was on the island when the children of Lir came.[59] It was he who said Mass when the children of Lir came.

Rope belt of St Francis. When a man is about to die, without a priest, St Francis appears to him and gives him the last rites.

‹ 18 September 1937. Fallmore ›

St[ephan] has for three days been turning the compass in every direction. Looks at the sky, moves the end of his long nose and says sententiously: If the wind stays to the north for two more days, the sea will grow calm little by little, little by little, and then you will be able to go to the island, maybe Sunday … But if the wind turns to the south, then things will take a turn for the worse (how they could get any worse in this elemental raging seems unimaginable). Maybe with a bit of luck … in three or four days … a boat will be able go out. But if the wind turns to the east …

This morning, things don't look too bad. Suddenly I see a currach off Goghtah.[60] I pounce on the opportunity: Why not us? St[ephan] looks at the

---

56 *Naomh Cearbhall ar* [St Cearbhall on]. St Cearbhall was a seventh-century Irish saint.　57 See p. 102, n. 63.　58 In the manuscript, the words '15th May arr' were crossed out and replaced by 'Comes back'. 59 See p. 47, n. 42. St Brendan here identified in lieu of St Mohévog or Kemoc.　60 Usual spelling: 'Gaghta', an island northeast of Duvillaun Beg. The etymology of this name refers to *geárrtha*, 'cut off' from the others.

sky, shakes his head. I sense that winds from every direction are about to descend on us again. I am deaf, deaf. N[orth], S[outh] or E[ast] no longer hold any weight for me. I must have a boat. St[ephan] nods, and transforms himself into a master of ceremonies charged with presenting a crew to us. Once pickaxe, spade and sieve have been assembled, he leaves, gravely, with us. At the crossroads, he hails a man who is passing on his donkey. The man accepts, gets down. He and St[ephan] disappear from the house in search of a second rower. St[ephan] reappears, goes down with us to the shore. Long wait. Finally, the two men appear. Middle-aged, stubborn, dumb faces, one has a prominent yellow tooth, and awkwardly passes two oar cleats from one hand to the other. The second man is holding a spade and looks at it stubbornly. He mutters: the weather doesn't look great. Yellow Tooth lifts his gaze, and the cleats. Knocked against each other, they make a sharp sound, and he stammers: I don't think we should touch the place where the saint is. – I swear to God that I will not touch the saint. His gaze falls again. Silence. St[ephan] rescues the situation with ease: I think that the weather really isn't great, you're right. But all the same we're going to go down as far as the jetty.

The crew, thus dismissed, go back up towards the village. St[ephan] shakes his head: they would have been good for nothing. Let's go to see the Inishkea people. Now his honour is at stake. The wind can blow from the north, from the south, it matters not at all to him. We will go, or he will lose face.

Hearing him call, a youngster from Inishkea sticks his head out from a currach that he is in the middle of fixing. With a sweep of the hand he is sent to the village, and returns accompanied by a big fellow with a merry smile.

6 o'clock. The squeaking of the oars in the cleats like a violin being tuned indefinitely. The silken swish of the sea on the prow. The black crests of the waves. Cormorants passing.

Shortly after disembarking, our crew rushes with pickaxe and spade ... to dig out rabbits. After half an hour spent taking photographs, we call them back, and they reappear triumphantly ... with five black rabbits.

Worked at the oratory.[61] We unearth its walls. The crew make tea. Then go back to hunting rabbits, even try to force them to race ... Worked again. The youngest, who has the face of a Greek god, a face that cannot smile, takes passionately to the trowel. Scratches. Scratches.[62]

---

61 This probably indicates the little church of St Colum Cille, called an 'oratory' in the 1838 Ordnance Survey. Henry also refers to it as the *teampull* [chapel].   62 In his letter of 2 June 1938, Harold Leask, Inspector of the National Monuments, writes to Françoise Henry to wish her good luck in her dig and imagines her 'burrowing and scratching rabbit fashion' (IVRLA, FHC, Stones/Sites/Notes relating to

❧ 19 September ❦

Inishkea. Worked for a long time on the kitchen midden. The crew scratches the sand as rabbits would, and digs up a crucifix. I scratch like a rabbit, and unearth some spirals. Many bones too, and shells, and white stones like eggs.

Tea in one of the houses. Showers, wind. We come back late. The sea is rough. No well-formed waves, but the water rising, swelling, then sinking, and the boat lifting, then diving into it, wavers and heads off again.

Black sea spangled with silver.

Duvillaun like a monster on the sea.

A mountain in a breaking cloud, pink, downy, shining with softness between the black sea and crimson sky.

Blazing cliffs of Achill.

A falcon[63] chasing a gull. They pass, and pass again. The gull dives, the falcon follows. They climb again. Suddenly separate. The gull sways for a moment like a dead leaf, then continues its flight.

Cliffs of Achill like a wall of Hell behind Duvillaun, caressed by a slanting ray. All the crests of the waves sparkling like glass.

Sprays of flame in the west.

A swan flying very far off, pitch-black against the fiery sky.

On the way here, each time the bow struck the waves, a spray of crystal spurting up like a shattered chandelier.

The rattle of plovers in the dunes.

❧ 20 September ❦

The crew refuses to go out on the sea. Wind, but not much undertow. They hide in the bakehouse.

Go down with Máire to Blacksod. The postmistress is very talkative.[64] I bring her a package to send for me, filled with bones from the kitchen middens.

She says to me: Somebody told me that you dug up the bones of the saint, and you took them away to put them in the cemetery.

---

the excavations at Inishkea County Mayo, image 28).   **63** In the manuscript, the word 'vulture' was deleted and replaced by the word 'falcon'.   **64** Françoise Henry returns to the postmistress' lack of discretion in a letter addressed to Adolf Mahr on 20 May 1939: 'Do not wire on any account, as the postmistress would at once make the contents of your wire public (it is the usual way ...)' (Archives, NMI, E63: L-L28 Inishkea North).

28 Bringing currachs on to the beach at Surgeview (Port Mór).

Hmm – M[áire] certainly saw the bones from the kitchen middens in my drawer the day Máirín[65] left. In a bad mood all day. If the postmistress – as is probable – opens my package, she is going to find tibias and she will not know that they are from cattle and wild boar ...

I tell her quite simply what is there, hoping in this way to flatter the smattering of learning on which she prides herself. Perhaps I succeed.

As for M[áire], I reflect a little on the way, then – like a good joke – tell her what Mrs S[weeney] said to me. I had been right to count on the hatred she feels for her. But my hopes are surpassed. If it was she who talked about the bones, she doesn't remember any more: one of her guests has been attacked.

The insult must be avenged by any means, the guest must be vindicated.

She spends the whole journey back telling me the misdemeanours of Mrs S[weeney],[66] who never pays her debts, and goes to Dublin to sell an elixir made with seawater and who knows what, that smells of rotten fish and which she claims cures cancer.

65 Máirín Bean Uí Dhálaigh, Henry's friend and member of team from the RIA preparing the *Dictionary of the Irish language*. She also calls her by her English name, Maureen, in this text.   66 Margaret Sweeney, with her husband Ted Sweeney, took care of the lighthouse as well as the post office in Blacksod. It was they who gave the forecast of stormy weather for 5 June 1944 that resulted in a 24-hour delay of plans

While I have my tea, I hear her telling the story of the bones to St[ephan], who laughs heartily. I had made vain efforts, which did not meet with approval, to take a boat to Achill. When I come back from the kitchen, I find St[ephan] there contemplating the sky through the open door, looking like an inspired oracle. M[áire] behind him, very excited, asks: Do you think the weather will be good, do you?

St[ephan] responds majestically: It may well be, if the wind keeps up. But if it turns to the south, I can't make any promises. In the end, it probably won't turn to the south. Then, turning to me, he says regally: I am going to find you a currach to go to Achill. If the weather keeps up, you can go easily. I stand there open-mouthed, then approve energetically. M[áire] becomes restless: Go on, go on St[ephan], take the donkey and go and ask ... A moment later St[ephan] comes out from the cowshed, and very solemnly, plants all two metres of himself on a diminutive donkey.

He comes back at nightfall with the news that Mr O'Moal,[67] the man with the yellow tooth, will take me tomorrow if the weather is good ...

---

for the Allies' landing on the Normandy beaches to 6 June. One of their sons is the lighthouse keeper today, though it has been fully automated.   **67** It is possible that here Françoise Henry heard the start of the Irish version of Lavelle family's name: Ó Maolfhabhail.

1938 journal[1]

❧ 7 June 1938 ❧

M[áire] informs me that a woman from Glosh, Ann Cawley, hearing talk of the expedition, declared that she would come with us: and I'll cook and bake bread for them, and I'll find wood for the fire. I accept enthusiastically. We go up the road of Glosh together. M[áire] sends a child to look for A[nn], who lives at the other end of the village. We negotiate in a house for our lodgings on the island. Then we go to M[c]F[adden]'s house. His forehead, nose and chin form equal projections from his head. Very talkative, in rather too flowery a manner. Not a very good impression. We go with him to the Captain's house.[2] A head like a bowling ball, with crinkling round eyes, a mouth the corners of which rise and fall in constant attempts to convey double meanings, a face that wrestles to express a superabundance of crazy ideas, jokes, changing impressions, a desperately sociable face, that wants to keep nothing to itself. He has worked out the whole expedition in his head: I will take a currach on the boat. And your provisions – and so on.

When the question of wages is raised, silence.[3]

1 The fourth notebook, 22 by 17.5cm, is untitled. It is listed as FH/B8/273 (4) (i) in the RIA archives. There are two typewritten transcriptions that Henry made of the first entries folded within the notebook. She changed the wording slightly in a few places; we have indicated these in the notes. 2 The 'Captain' is difficult to name. Pat Cheit Lavelle, son of 'the admiral' and father to John and Dominic, who had their photo taken with the swan, shared the job of delivering the mail from the lighthouse at Blackrock with John Padden via motorboat. Another possibility would be Antoine Tommy Ó Maoineacháin, one of two who survived the 1927 storm (see pp 64–5, n. 19) and who may be the Anthony Muirnachan that Henry calls 'captain' on 12 August 1946. Although Henry seems to have tried to record names very carefully, it is easy to confuse 'Maoineacháin' (Meenaghan) and 'Muirnacháin' (Monaghan), especially since the two families intermarried. She also identifies 'the captain' as the uncle of her young employee, Seánin Ó Maoineacháin, on 2 July 1938. According to the way relatives were figured by the islanders, Antoine Tommy would not have been a blood uncle, however, for Henry, the fact that he was married to the sister of Seánin's mother might have been enough. Of course, Henry also uses 'captain' (lower case 'c') when referring to whoever is piloting a boat or acting as a leader, so the references may be too entangled to sort this one identification. 3 The variant, in a typewritten version of the first four and a half pages of this black notebook (FH/B8/273 (4) (ii)–(iii)), reads as follows: 'is raised, and when we indicate the official rate, there is a long silence'.

M[c]F[adden][4] declares in an indignant tone that he will never work for such a rate.[5] Do I know the price of a loaf of bread? Do I know what life is like in such a place? And so on and so forth. 10 shillings, no less. I reply very coldly that I am not the one who sets the prices, that plenty of people in the centre [capital], where things cost more, are happy to get 5 shillings a day. I take out the sheet from the Land Commission. The Captain, who has worked on some relief schemes, clearly finds it all very reasonable. M[cFadden] looks down his nose at it, and starts speaking English, which is always a bad sign.[6] We all go back out together. At his gate, M[cFadden] leaves us, saying: I'll see you again soon.

Máire is indignant. A storm of remarks. 10 shillings!!! In the evening, Ann arrives, having found three men: a father and son, and the lad who was in the Captain's house. There is still the question of turf.

The whole day of the 8th [of June] spent on orders and counter-orders. No house available on the north island. Will we have to go to the south island? In any case, the storm is raging, no way to cross.

On the morning of the 9th [of June], Ann announces that the father and his son have left for Glasgow on the morning bus ... But she is going to find someone, of course. A moment later, the Captain arrives. Mr McFadden says now that he would ask no more than to come after all.[7] But it is I who am no longer interested. And I think they are not displeased that I am holding firm. Around 11 o'clock, Stephan calls me to 'show' me two lads between 18 and 20 years old who nudge each other and chuckle: Will they not do the job? I

---

4 Note the varying names used to designate John McFadden: Seán Mac Faidín, John Padden.   **5** This is only the first of a series of wrangles between John McFadden and Françoise Henry over finances. Having received £5 for the incomplete transfer of the stone slabs in 1938, he requested £10 for the same project in 1939, taking into account the weight of the slabs and above all the risk of hostility from his neighbours. Showing herself, for once, somewhat unsympathetic towards the boatman's delicate situation, Françoise Henry accused him of 'blackmail'. In a letter to Adolf Mahr, dated 20 May 1939, she encourages him to write a strongly worded letter to John McFadden: 'he goes on piling up lies in a way which makes me suspect that he is simply trying to blackmail you' (Archives, NMI, E63: L-L28 Inishkea North). In the end, John McFadden received £7 in 1939.   **6** This suggests that all, including Henry, were speaking Irish.   **7** In the typewritten version that Henry made of this text, she inserted some clarification. The 'Captain' tells her that McFadden will do it after all. This explains the receipt, dated the 9 June 1938, signed by Seán Mac Faidín, for £3 10s., being the price of hiring a motorboat to transport the archaeologist and her crew to the island: 'Received from Mlle Françoise Henry the sum of £3 10s. for hire of motorboat to take her, the people who are going to work on the excavation, a load of turf and various provisions to Inishkea North./June 9th 1938/Seán Mac Faidín' (IVRLA, FHC, Stones/Sites/Notes relating to the excavations at Inishkea County Mayo, image 27). Françoise Henry's small ledger also notes '£3 10s. Boat, Seán Mac Faidín, June 9th' (IVRLA, FHC, Stones/Sites/Notes relating to the excavations at Inishkea County Mayo, image 93).

approve enthusiastically. Suddenly, things happen at a dizzying pace. I hardly have time to gather our provisions before the boat is passing offshore outside our windows, while real gypsy furnishings accumulate in the wheelbarrow. There are a frying pan, saucepans, a pot, a broom and so on. The lads grab my suitcase and some baskets;[8] a bundle of blankets appears from somewhere. Áine runs over with a sieve, some shovels and pickaxes appear. We go down the road towards the shore and the quay. Half of the male population of Glosh is leaning against one of the hookers beached high on the shore. They watch us pass without comment. Ann arrives, brandishing a milk jug half wrapped in a piece of brown paper. M[áire][9] discovers all of a sudden that she has forgotten the plates and sends Áine to get them. Where is the flour? A child runs off looking for it. The little motor boat sits proudly in the middle of the bay, among a bustling mass of currachs.[10] Two chairs, some sacks of turf and the luggage are hoisted up.[11] A little donkey appears, trotting, the sack of flour on its back, scolded by the child. Áine hurtles down the road in a din of crockery.

We finally hoist ourselves onto the deck among the chairs and turf. The captain[12] has piled up the rest in the hold, any old how. A currach appears, bringing our two lads and an old man whose nose is in the shape of a potato, with shifty eyes and a bushy moustache.[13] Ann, seated beside me on a sack of turf, whispers: He's coming too, a very good worker, you'll see.

Finally, we weigh anchor. The sea is still rough. A currach is hoisted on board. Maureen,[14] Ann and I, squeezed between its planks and the sacks of turf, completely cover the tarred area of the boat. Ann announces that she is going to be seasick, and wraps herself with everything in reach, a jersey that she ties around her head, some coats, a piece of sacking. She is still holding in one hand her milk jug, the paper around which is coming undone.

Fast and choppy crossing. In less than half an hour we are in the little bay,[15] between the ruined village and the Bailey Mór.[16] A new transshipment. The

8 In the manuscript, the following version was deleted: 'a bag of baskets'.   9 This M could also refer to Maureen, who also had a list of provisions. It is unclear.   10 In a letter addressed to Adolf Mahr, director of the NMI, dated 12 June 1938, Françoise Henry gives an account of the means of transport for going from the mainland to the island: either the 'lighthouse motor boat: expensive (£3 10s.), takes only half an hour, rocks a lot' or a '*currach* (from £1 to £2, be firm). Take at least an hour, rocks pleasantly …' (Archives, NMI, E63: L-L28, Inishkea North).   11 In the same letter as that cited in the preceding note, Françoise Henry informs Adolf Mahr that 'the lighthouse boat is probably calling tomorrow with turf for us […]'.   12 In this case, she is referring to McFadden, who is 'captaining' the boat.   13 This is Pat Reilly, who would be about 59, since Henry mentions that he is 71 when he continues to work for her in 1950.   14 See p. 57, n. 66.   15 The Porteen Beg.   16 Bailey Mór, large sand dune in Inishkea North.

29 View from motorboat in bay towards north island village, taken while transferring to a currach for landing.

30 View from boat in bay towards north island village. In the centre are all that remains of the houses shown in Henry's photograph, above (photograph by Janet Marquardt, June 2011).

various objects that were heaped up in the hold are taken out higgledy-piggledy,[17] and transferred to the currach before finally ending up on the little beach.

We climb up through the village, and eventually stop beside the house at the top, a relatively tidy looking house, with a slate roof, a door and almost all the glass still in its windows. With determination, Ann undoes the rope holding the door shut; the men force the piece of wood that serves as a lock. And shamelessly we take possession of it. There is a large kitchen, with slightly blue-tinted, white-washed walls, which are peeling. Laboriously, the fisherman have written and rewritten their names and addresses in pencil here and there. There are even a few attempts at drawing, a duck, a woman's profile and laboured quotations of poems learned at school. The wall over the chimney has lost its plaster and displays its naked brickwork in the middle of some brownish cement.

Two bedrooms with wooden floors, clean, apart from a few spiders' webs.

We move in. I dig out a piece of lobster tank behind a house, which, perched on two pieces of crate, makes an open-weave table. The lads bring another piece of jetsam, which they set on some stones to make another table. An upturned basket serves as a seat, a tea chest as another. Ann directs operations, arranges our beds on the ground of one of the wooden-floored bedrooms – big blankets and a red flannel counterpane. For her own, she unrolls three sacks of straw, which she places before the fire. The men, in the end bedroom, are accommodated much like us.

We have hardly gone to bed before an upheaval begins outside: pushing, pressing, panting. A moo starts up, hesitatingly. Another responds, questioningly; sharp miaows, a bray, then another, in that frantic tone adopted by donkeys. It seems that all the domestic animals of the island have passed on the news to each other: There is an inhabited house. They come, press up against the walls, breathe heavily at the windows, push their big muzzles against the panes, call, beg. Finally, with a push, the door opens, and the head of an alarmed heifer, almost a calf, is framed in the opening. Ann bustles about and shouts, hurling imprecations mixed with exclamations of tenderness: Good little calf, hey, get on with you, poor thing, out! Hoosh, get out of there. Go on, go on, my sweet!

The men.[18] P[at], whose face seems to have been stretched out by being pinched at the forehead and chin. It was not possible, for all that, to bring out

---

Biolla: 'sand dune' in Irish (see Rita Nolan, *Within the Mullet*, p. 24). **17** The manuscript page that begins here is a separate sheet (FH/B8/273 (4) (iv)), clipped to the corresponding page in the black notebook (FH/B8/273 (4) (i)). **18** The manuscript page that begins here (*recto* and *verso*) is a separate

31 Former 'Sweeney House', on the left, rented from Joe Sweeney of Achill, where Henry lived during the excavations. The building on the right is the former National School. Both have had their windows and roofs replaced (photograph by Janet Marquardt, June 2011).

any distinct feature in it. His eyes disappearing in a bushy tangle of hairs, his mouth in another, his nose somewhat prominent. Always tries to squeeze a bit more out of you than is needed, but works hard. As much a poser as the rest of them when it comes to picking up an oar, is afraid of coming back in a storm, takes the dole while working here. But he has a certain good-natured shrewdness, endless stories about all his contemporaries, which he tells to the two lads while working. A certain interest in his work, when it is explained to him what is going on.

S[eán], his son, very much a boy still maturing from many points of view, but a certain kindness, a sort of innate courtesy.

S[eán]ín. His father drowned in the disaster ten years ago.[19] Degenerate blood, red eyes, double thumb. He doesn't seem very strong, but works like a

sheet (FH/B8/273 (4) (v)), clipped to the corresponding page in the black notebook (FH/B8/273 (4) (i)). The receipts preserved in the IVRLA FHC (UCD) allow us to confirm the anglicized names of the father and son in question: Patrick and John Reilly. See also 2 July for the arrival of Peter Reilly.   **19** On 28 October 1927, a horrible storm took the lives of forty-five fishermen from the west coast of Ireland. Ten were from the Inishkeas. Thirty men went out in the afternoon from the islands during what seemed

32 Ann and some of the men watching a cow from the doorway of the 'Sweeney House'.

devil. Always playing jokes. About 12 years old and claims to be 20. His voice is breaking. Wild laugh. A puppy type of unruliness. P[at] is his whipping boy. He is forever pulling his leg, then, when the old man has fallen into the trap, doubles up laughing. Impossible to know what S[eán] makes of it.

∽ 10 June ∾

Walk around the shore with Ann. She wanders here and there, picks up a glass ball a little farther on, then brandishes a piece of mast all bleached from

perfect weather. After storm signs appeared, most of the older men turned back while the younger men stayed out in six, two-man, *currachs* to cast their nets a second time. They were caught in the worst of the storm and only one crew, the brothers John and Anthony Meenaghan, survived, being cast up on the mainland. It is said that this event took the heart out of the remaining people on the islands and they moved to the mainland. Of course, there were other reasons – they had become more dependent upon the state over the years and had no resident healthcare provider on the islands. The clergy also wanted them to regularly attend church and save the priests the trouble of coming over to the islands to say Mass as well as make it possible for them to obtain last rites and consecrated burials. The government helped them relocate and provided land. Seánín was the son of Seán Meenaghan, the only married man who drowned; one of seven children left to his widowed mother.

33 'Very small, huddled against the ground, packets of down living only by their frightened eyes'.

having been washed up by the sea. Then calls us loudly to show us a gull's nest: three yellowy eggs speckled with a diluted black, like marble that had been dipped in oil. 'I'll tame them when they're out of the egg', and she marks the nest with a pile of pebbles. Various other pieces of wood. The smooth shore bears the imprint of birds' feet. Seaweed lies about, wrinkled and blistered like sloughed snake skins – countless hydras, hydras killed by some superhuman Hercules, because related to the great blue and gold rocks which rise down there by the sea.[20] A slimy, multi-headed hydra, terrifyingly marine. Nothing like that papier-mâché monster killed by S[aint] M[ichael] in the manner of Carpaccio.[21]

Higher up in the low grass, a small tuft of immobile feathers, a black beak stuck to the ground. In the sky, panicked bird-cries. A tiny little thing, its black skin appearing at the stumps of its wings. Cowers a little in the hand,[22] then escapes and runs, long stilts and bunches of feathers flailing grotesquely.

20 Original version: 'which float down there'. 21 Here it appears that Henry simply mistakenly wrote the word '*depuis*' when she meant '*d'après*' Vittore Carpaccio, *Saint George and the dragon* (Venice, *c*.1504). 22 In the manuscript, there here appears in the margin the word *vannelle* (an unconventional spelling of *vanneau*): 'lapwing'.

34 Ann holding two chicks, 'yellowy, spotted with black'.

Two others in a small hollow, yellowy, spotted with black. Very small, huddled against the ground, packets of down living only by their frightened eyes.[23] Further on, in the rock graves near which lie some white, stripped bones, oyster-catcher nests. And the mother whirling, her red beak out in front, with rapid flapping of wings.[24] The dark blue sea seems to retain a little of the sunlight accumulated during the day; under a pale sky where the whites and greys of formless clouds grow sharper.

Right at the end of the island, beside the channel, the shining back of a currach, bustling figures. Two men just back from fishing, struggling with the soles that they want to thread along a string. A curling, gleaming white belly, and flapping tail. Browns spotted with red shining in a last ray of sun. They come back up with us, one swinging his string of silvery leaves, the other a gutted pollock with its entrails and greenish mouth showing.

The swans float among the irises of the lake. The dull noise of the sea rises from all around, lapwings[25] pass by, dead leaves sent into a spin by the rattle of the wind. The men talk about their catch, and the French trawler anchored down near the Carraig Dubh.[26] Strange that they can read the English papers

23 In the margin of the manuscript, there here appears the word *pluviers*: 'plovers'.　24 In the original, *des flappements d'ailes précipités*, where the English verb undoubtedly displaced the French *battements* to produce the neologism *flappements*.　25 *Vannelles*, unconventional spelling of *vanneaux*. Original version, *pluviers* ('plovers').　26 See p. 30, n. 4.

and yet do not speak English? The hospitality of the French boats where the rum flows ...

This evening, the pale blue sea and the big slate mountains set on it beneath a white moon not yet bright. The great silence of the hour when the birds are asleep. The tranquillity in which sleeps the vague awareness of the storm to come, a sort of motionless waiting. Our men have gone to visit the fishermen in the house down below. The heifers bump faintly against each other behind the door. A large silhouette blocks the square of silvery light. The bigger of the sole fishers comes in, brushing his chest ... Then the smaller, bouncing a little. They sit down on two chairs. Áine welcomes them, bustling about. Maureen and I sit down on some sacks, our backs to the wall on either side of the fire. Áine puts a candle in the window.[27]

❧ 11 June ❧

Achill has vanished. The ghost of Duvillaun floats on an iridescent sea. The horn of the Eagle Island lighthouse bellows in the fog.[28] The world seems to have become unreal beyond this grassy rock where the sea breaks dully. Went down with A[nn] right to the end of the island. She wanted to go over to the other side of the sound, but the currach has gone, fishing somewhere in the depths of the mist.

The sound is striped with crimson and pale blue-green, which fades into transparency on the sand. Bird-prints on the beach like tiny anchors. The decomposing amethyst of sea anemones. Beyond a few black rocks at the entrance to this almost closed bay, the sea bubbles and hurls angry jets, very white. Three, four, five seals play among the seaweed in the bay. Triangular head, black on the greenish water. Sometimes a whole silhouette, like a half mushroom. Then it vanishes. Reappears a little nearer, its eyes level with the water, questioning. A big, gleaming dog's head. Dives and snorts. We watch them for a long time, half hidden among the granite rocks dotted with patches of gold and silver lichen, sprouting rough, grey mosses, between which tremble tufts of sea-pink, purple, pink, whitish.

---

27 The Irish tradition of placing a lighted candle in the window relates specifically to Christmas Eve and is intended as a welcome to Mary and the Holy Family. By extension, it has become a welcome to all strangers at all times of the year.　28 In 1835, two lighthouses were operational on Eagle Island, which is situated northwest of Belmullet, where the Atlantic rages, but only one lighthouse remains today.

35 The Dock, which Henry calls the 'Drak' or 'Drack' (see p. 75, n. 35) (photograph by Brian Dornan, June 2009).

36 Seals at the Dock (photograph by Sean Lavelle, March 2009).

37 The piece of *giúsach* used as a chair in the house with Ann preparing food,
a cigarette hanging from her lips.

Only twenty years since the sea cut off the far end of the island. There was, where the bay is now, a kitchen midden almost as big as the one here that was gradually washed away.

Áine and I were waiting for Maureen. We see her suddenly appear against the sky, haloed by her sou'wester, holding a large plank, streaming water. A little further on appears Pat, who was looking for her, swaying nonchalantly beside the two fishermen. A[nn] watches from the doorway, and exclaims: They've no fire in their house! I say to her: Call them, they'll have their tea with us. She returns, brandishing three enormous crab claws. They send you that and thank you: We'll busy ourselves preparing the tea, cutting big slices of bread, frying bacon. Willie and the monkey arrive. They sit at the table, gulping down the food. Pat, very satisfied, presides over the ceremony, sitting at the edge of the other 'table'. After a moment, Willie[29] swings his legs over the other side of the crate that he is using as a chair, the monkey moves his crate away from the table. With their elbows on their knees, their faces faintly lit by a glimmer from the fire, they discuss the day's catch, which was bad, the

29 In the manuscript, the word 'Willie' is preceded by crossed-out words, *ils se retournent*, 'they turn back around' (see also p. 85, n.50).

38 Possibly Pat Reilly sitting on the *giúsach* 'chair'.

seals in the bay, a sign of a storm, and praise the features of the islet, which we were unable to reach today. There is a room cut into the rock, there, you'll see, everything is made of stone. Pat nods his head: apparently once, long ago, three murderers from the Norwegian island hid themselves there. But the soldiers came, took one and then another, but the third stayed hidden for a long time.[30]

Outside, the sociable animals are gathering. From time to time, a damp black muzzle appears at the door, big humble eyes and the end of an ear shaped like a round paddle.

At the far end of the room, near the bedroom door, there is a big piece of *giúsach*,[31] a strange silvery trunk, like satin, bristling with stumps, a remnant

30 This anecdote may refer to one dating to the Viking period. The islanders tell the story of a girl killed in the island by the 'Lochlannaigh' [Scandinavians]. Henry's use of the term 'island' for Norway is odd, but she was reporting the men's words.   31 'Bog deal' or a common Irish wood preserved in a peat bog.

39 Cow at the posts ('pickets') that were being erected to create a barrier against the beasts' destructive interventions in the excavations.

of a submerged forest washed up from Achill by the sea. It shimmers gently in the last gleam of daylight falling from the doorway. A white glint clings to a basin. The jumble of sacks and brooms in the corner has something cosy about it, gives the impression of a well-furnished house.

How does Maureen come to ask Willie: Have you ever seen a mermaid?[32] W[illie], who has twice been to America, shakes his head: Not I, but she has (pointing to Áine). Yes, she says, one day I saw her on the shore, and she was combing her hair. Pat screws up his hollow face: I've seen one, too. She had red hair, a big clump of it, like that, and he makes as big a fist as he can with his knobbly fingers. Maur[een]: If you take their bonnet, do they stay on the land? – Maybe so, but it's not a bonnet they have, it's a sort of hood, a red one. Like a big pendulum, the head of a cow, which is scratching its neck on the doorpost, appears and disappears, rhythmically. A donkey's mane, bristling from the rain, looks like the fin of a fish.

The schoolmaster who put a pebble on each boy's knee, and beat him if the stone fell. Comes here and doesn't want to believe in ghosts. Meets some cows on a stormy, snowy night, when nobody would leave an animal outside.

32 See p. 47, n. 43.

Around 11 o'clock, Willie[33] suddenly gets up. The monkey, as if gathering his scattered limbs, a lock of hair over his eyes, makes the same movement. They go off into the night. A moment later our two lads return, having drunk their tea in the third inhabited house, the one above the harbour.

A[nn]: We're much better off on the island now. Before there were people everywhere. Now you can go where you want without worrying about anyone. And then there are all the birds!

She brings us our tea at 11 o'clock in the morning, on the dig. We sit down at the foot of the big stone slab. M[aureen] drops her bread in the mud. That doesn't matter, says A[nn]: *Beith sé le na duinne mairebh* [*Bíodh sé seo le haghaidh na ndaoine marbha*: 'Let this be for the dead people'], and throws it towards the slab.

These animals certainly have a passion for everything human.

Panic at the dig this morning: a heifer has taken the ruler, which sticks out of her mouth like a giant cigarette. Another has taken the surveying rope in her teeth and goes off proudly, her head out in front, dragging the rope and pickets with her. A third rubs herself with delight against the wheelbarrow. Very young animals, hardly weaned from the bucket of potatoes and milk. They follow Pat, who is coming back from the well with a bucket of water, a stubborn hope in their eyes.

This morning, one of them put her nose so insistently against the door that A[nn] could not resist. She gathers potato skins, tosses them with a little water in a bucket. The animal eats, greedily, then wants to take everything in the house, the bread on the table, the fish on a crate, and so on.

The *neamhóg*.

A[nn] going out, a basin of water on her hip, and before throwing it out the door: Took, tchook, tchook, ook, ook … as if calling the ghost of chickens past.

The other island. An inhabited house. An old man and his two daughters.[34] Him, a strange, wrinkled and hairy schoolboy's face, sea-blue eyes that look out at you from beneath the peak of his cap. Them: a little Maggie with a funny elastic face which tenses and slackens into laughs and grimaces, a nose

33 In the manuscript, the words 'and the monkey', after 'Willie', were deleted.   34 The Antoine Tommy Ó Maoineacháin family on Inishkea South. Maggie married Michael O'Meenaghan (different family, same name: see p. 59, n. 2) and Eileen married Sean Reilly.

40 Possibly Maggie, seen at one of the western inlets with steep cliffs.

that seems mobile. Eileen, fine features in an oval face, a little pointed towards the chin, a slightly short upper lip that gives her a certain haughtiness, huge eyes of the same blue as her father's, hair in a pageboy style, a large red jumper rolled at the neck, a green skirt and a black apron which she makes into a shawl while walking.

Climbed to the top of the hill. From there, suddenly this island, which seemed gentler than ours, appears a cataclysm. Desperate struggle of the sea and this rock it slams against. Granite schist hewn by the raging sea's clubbing blows into great slabs. Below us, very far down, there is nothing but rocks heaped on the bare stone, bristling at the water today so calm. Two or three large rocky outcrops set against the open sea. Between them, splits that will open one day into a channel.

We go down the slope. Loud cries of Áine as soon as M[aggie] comes near the rocks. *A Thiarna, a Mhuire!* ['Saviour, Mary!'] She tries to gather us in as if we were cows. The hill on the sea side bursts open in a black wound. Large slopes of ebony and mahogany coloured granite striped with vertical fissures.

Walked for a long time among the rocks. Arrived opposite one of the tops of the rocky outcrops. Black rocks, as if cut with a knife. Swaying of the sea, which foams on the rocks, then lightly, effortlessly, rises. The instant when

41 Ann, probably Maggie and Eileen, maybe Maureen.

the sparkling foam is no more than a cloud hesitating in the sun, before falling back slowly as snow. In the light, the sea before me seems almost black, the blue-black of clear, moonless nights. Achill blue too, softly wrapped up in clouds.

The Drak.[35] There is a cave in the cliff, which opens a little further on into a gaping hole in the surface of the islet. We watch the dark transparent sea there, where the submerged rocks gleam white. Throw pebbles. From the depths of the rock some muffled roars respond. We lean in closer: the cave

---

35 The west sides of the islands have many of these rocky inlets with steep cliffs where the ocean spray and foam collects and seals gather at the mouth. The one that Henry describes often in these pages and calls 'the Drak' (or in 1950 'Drack') is on the far north end of Inishkea North, where a tidal zone cuts off access to the island tip at all times except low tide. It is now known as 'the Dock'. It may be that Henry misunderstood the pronunciation and thought it was an Irish word she was transcribing phonetically like 'draec' (pronounced 'drach') or even 'drac', which has fallen into disuse in today's Irish, but which, according to the *Dictionary of the Irish language: based mainly on Old and Middle Irish materials* (known as the DIL and available online), signified 'fire', possibly by relation to the association between 'fire' and 'dragon'. This hypothesis would fit with the cave's identity as a place giving forth foam or shooting spray, like a dragon breathing fire. It may also be that the current usage of 'dock' is a corruption of the original word she was hearing. However, according to Brian Dornan, there is an area here where islanders once docked *currachs*. It is also a major breeding location for grey seals. Her earlier description of this area, which she calls 'the end of the island', describes it as a 'sound' or 'bight' (*le bras de mer*) and an 'almost closed bay': see beginning of same entry for 11 June.

42 View of a western inlet ('Calf Cove'), with 'two or three rocky outcrops set against the open sea'.

continues into darkness, very far below the islet. Seals hidden in its depths must have heard us.

Incredible weather. An evening with the sun full over the rocks of Achill. Granite also, no doubt. Sparkling in the sun, above a sea the colour of dark blue velvet. These evenings when gradually cliffs and mountains become more and more unreal, from blue turn slowly to incredible pink hues, shades of dying embers where redness can be seen beneath silvery ashes. Then that slow subsidence of colours. Those tones, which empty themselves of all strength, while the ever clearer sea still dreams of the vanished light.

❧ 16 June ❧

A grey morning. Big gulls in groups on the sand, laboriously trying to get up when we pass. Pat remarks: They're taking shelter. Sign of a storm. Later, Seán points out the seals passing, sheltered by the island. And they begin to sing in their mournful groan. Murky sky, notable greenish slits in the confusion of clouds, faint sulphurous glows here and there. Despondency weighs on everything. The black-headed gulls sway on the sea. Even the lapwing almost forgets to unleash its rattle.

43 Three men and a woman launching a currach.

North island for Dev.[36] South island for Cosgr[ave]. 'Great sport' during the Troubles.[37] The men of the north [island] flying the republican flag at the summit of the B[ailey] Mór. Those of the south [island] coming to tear it down during the night. Two days later, it mysteriously reappears at the summit of the south island.

✎ 18 June ✎

Pat had asked for a morning off ... to claim his unemployment allowance at Blacksod. He swears he will be back for lunch. With the excuse that he has waited for my post, reappears calmly at a quarter past 5. Makes a few half-hearted attempts at digging.

On the eve of Corpus Christi,[38] the lads having announced that they were going to spend the day on land, I pay everyone. To Pat, I give a half-day for his expedition – considering that already quite generous. He takes it very badly, and in the end informs me that he and his son will leave on Saturday. I reply

36 Éamon de Valera.   37 Referring to the Irish War of Independence, 1919–21, leading to the Anglo-Irish Treaty of 1921, after which de Valera and Cosgrave formed the two rival political parties, Fianna Fáil and Fine Gael.   38 Latin for 'Body of Christ' and referring to the Christian feast day celebrated on the first Thursday after the season of Easter ends, which varies from late May to late June.

that it is all the same to me – which is actually quite true. Ann, furious, declares that she will find someone else. I would not be far from finishing the excavations on Saturday. But there is Seánín who must be relying on next week. I tell Ann that I will keep him on if he wants to stay, and I let events take their course. Today, at lunch, Ann asks Seán: Are you coming back on Monday? Seán, with a sidelong glance at his father, replies: But yes, of course. I am sure that Ann has taken someone else on, so that I find myself with three workers once more, and it is Pat who is a little sheepish.

Shouts and exclamations when I declare my intention to stay: You can't stay all alone on the island! – And why not? – In the faces that turn to look at me, I can read the reply that they dare not make. Instead they say, unconvincingly: If there were a storm, what would you do? I gesture in amusement towards the provisions: Do you think I am in danger of starving? You can't stay on your own like that. I go right to the heart of the matter: Think of the good time I'll have with all the ghosts who will come to see me. They'll be all around the fire. I look around. A sort of relief. So I thought of the ghosts. After all, maybe they're no risk to me. All the same ... Ann, seized by an idea, goes down towards the houses. She comes running back. Pat, Tom and Seán say that they will probably spend the weekend here. You'll be all right.

– So there's no harm in my staying alone on the island with two fishermen. But alone with the ghosts!!

In the end, the fisherman decide to go. But my people get used to the idea. Ann, who wanted to stay, lets herself be persuaded. As a concluding argument, I say to her: But of course, there have only ever been nice people on the island, so there can only be very nice *Taïvshe* [*Taidhbhse*: 'ghosts']? – That's true. – So, I will make them very welcome, and everything will go splendidly. (When you think of the pirate bands and shipwreckers who must have lived here ...).

The currach leaves, Pat, Seán and Maureen rowing. Seánín and I push it out to sea. A wave lifts it, and it goes off, Seánín kneeling on the stern, making faces. Farewell waves, a few jokes that are lost in the wind. And I am alone.

Strange that this ruined village is not more melancholy. A kind of pervading gentleness. I walk around the island. Absurd oyster-catchers clinging to the cliff-edge, chattering with loud clacks of their red beaks, then taking off heavily all of a sudden, and gliding, black and white dominoes spread out above the blue-green sea.

44 'Near the village, I meet the herd, which is slowly migrating'.

No seals by the Dún.[39] Is this a sign that the weather is going to get better? Gusts of warm fog turning into fine droplets in the wind. The sea shining white on the rocks, then disappearing in the soft, grey atmosphere. The little gulls have all left their nest. There are still a few oyster-catcher eggs here and there, between the stone slabs. Further on, I almost walk on a small lapwing in the grass. Crouched on the ground at my approach, its beak horizontal, it is a black and beige ball, hardly visible flat against the earth. The mother whirls in the sky with piercing calls. When I walk away, the creature gets up and flees, its stumpy wings beating against its sides. Donkeys huddled in a break in the dune for shelter.

Near the village, I meet the herd, which is slowly migrating. They come from all around, with stubborn steps. Their big eyes gaze at me, imploringly, as if they had already realized that I was now their only link with humanity. They gather before the door, solemn, mute, almost tragic. When I shut it in their faces, they start to push against it, with muffled snorts, and a big muzzle appears at the window, trying to see through the opaque glass. I am obliged

39 This is an area Henry believes was once a promontory fort, or 'dun', near what she calls the 'Drak' (see p. 75, n. 35) where birds have always nested in the grass. It is north of Doon Lough. See Henry, 'Remains of the Early Christian period on Inishkea North', p. 206 in the Pindar ed.

to go and speak to them. I throw them some lettuce leaves, which they sniff noisily. Then doubtless satisfied with this sign of attention on my part, they drift off slowly, pushing each other, advancing and retreating, sometimes going back on their steps again. Until finally there remains just one donkey with a mischievous look, foraging right and left, and some birds swooping in a returning beam of sunlight.

Went out for a moment. The fog comes apart in grey clouds that roll on the sea. Flights of gulls rise, black, on the scallop-pink sky. A gale rises from the open sea and beats like a sail. The sea drools on the rocks; sometimes a spurt of foam shoots up. A delayed lapwing moans around the chapel of Colum Cille.

In the still half-light of the house, the fire glows red and murmurs secrets to the purring kettle. Three yellow irises in a condensed milk tin on the windowsill have something comical about them. The wind breaks above the hill and rolls in dull waves over the house.

The *taïvshe*? Who could they be? Some of those wild monks who wandered with St Brendan on the unknown sea and celebrated Easter each year on the back of a whale? Old sea-dogs who camped on the islet between two raids? Poor fishermen stalked by famine and working out how to hold on until the next cast of the net?

The two holes in the corrugated iron around the window.

Around midnight, it is not the *taïvche* who came, but the storm, the sound of a flapping sail, these tremors of the walls and roof, which, as I am half asleep, give me an illusion of sliding endlessly in a boat fleeing before the wind. Clack, clack. Is it one of those jet-black sails of the *poukauns*[40] of Connemara, dyed with tar, and heavy in the wind? There are whistles and creaks, like rigging under strain.

But this sound of pots banging, this mooing? Ahead of the storm, the worried herd turned back to the house. They bump against the sheet of corrugated iron that blocks the door, push, snort, call. The house is assailed by an upheaval of livestock, by a sound of scratching hooves, by large masses brushing against the walls. Then disorderly stampedes, and the sobbing fanfare of the donkeys.

40 See p. 129, n. 36.

❧ 19 June ❧

This morning, clear sun and raging wind. Still misty on the land side. On the open water, an indigo sea shimmering up to a hard line at the edge of the sky. Green and white spirals whirling around the rocks. The promontories of the south island are black in a crown of dazzling foam. The sky is light, moving and infinite. A powerful joy in the air.

Lit the fire. Went down to get water from the well. Tidied and swept the house, which needed it badly.

Went out again around 1 o'clock. A harsh wind that passes flat over the sea and land, scraping, biting. The sea bubbles around the rocks but does not manage to rise up again. Black, fermenting with quiet rage. At times the horizon clouds over, gusts of spray pass by in a more furious wind. Cairrig Dubh[41] and the south island blur, disappear, absorbed in a tumultuous atmosphere. Then patches of molten silver reappear on the sea, the ghost of Achill slowly emerges, the foam turns once again to a hard white.

7 o'clock. The sea now is raging. The big breakers form and rush in from the open water, swell, and then crumble on the rocks. Huge rolling waves swell in a whiteness lined with an intense green, then, with great roars, rise like trees of snow. The cracks of the rock bubble as if with the foam from a diabolical laundry. Waves jump and hurl themselves onto it, tear apart on the ridges of the black walls, hiss, crash and blend back into the yellowish muck. The sun, wild too, strikes the waves with gold and silver blows, heightens the geysers of foam to the most implausible limits of blinding white.

A turbulent, thrilling happiness in all this raging. The same oppression of an immense force of nature as when the cliffs of Achill appear too clearly in all their immensity, covered in oppressively fantastical colours.

10 o'clock. Setting sun. A pale yellow sun from which fall a few great ghostly rays, and that is about to disappear among heavy grey masses that weigh on the sea. Deathly pale clouds roll towards Achill, which is slowly disappearing. Large jets of foam still mark the rocks of Duvillaun, which can hardly be made out. The wind, which had weakened a little, redoubles its strength, becomes brutal, unrelenting. The gulls, sitting heavily on the ground, draw their heads into their shoulders.

This island of calm that is the house, tucked well in against the hill, presenting only a blank wall to the blows of the wind, warm from the light of

---

41 See p. 30, n. 4.

45 Henry's only surviving photograph where one can make out the head of a seal. She was renowned among her colleagues as a terrible photographer, expecting the darkroom technician at UCD to correct with exposure and contrast.

a candle and the glimmer of the live embers. From the window, I can still make out the white foam that surrounds the rocks even on this side, and very far away, a faint grey curve crowned by its tower,[42] the hill of Glosh, from where one perhaps can see a light. Solitude becomes a reality, thrilling.

❧ 20 June ❧

The wind, still raging, though perhaps a little less strong. I examine my provisions. There would be enough for a month! Except perhaps turf, and there would always be the option of burning the floorboards of an abandoned house.

The sea now raging. It is no longer stiffened by too strong a wind. It has taken on its full volume, its ease of movement. The furious animals of the open sea, white manes to the wind, rush onto the rocks. Rising foam that

42 A square watchtower on the summit of Termon Hill, 53m above sea level. It is not the same design as the famous round Martello towers built across England and along the coast of Ireland, but was also meant to guard against a possible invasion by Napoleon (see colour pl. 9).

46 Doon Lough.

blooms in huge flourishes, shines iridescent, hesitates, and collapses in cascades. What potentate could allow himself the dissolute luxury of these fountains! Great gushing walls which suddenly capitulate, cataracts, and a solitary jet that spurts out at times from a crevasse. The joy of being alone with that. Too immense for a human presence. Wandered for a long time on this giant's staircase that borders the island on the west. Came back opposite the Drak. In the gully, a big grey seal was bathing.

The inveterate curiosity of the seals. One looks right at me, his two big eyes level with the water. Dives. Then he reappears for me to admire his hook-nosed profile. And then, squeezed in as much as possible, he lifts himself halfway out of the water, as if standing on tiptoe, and shows, beneath his round head, his shoulders spotted with white, like those of a tattooed human. The click of my camera puts him to flight, and I see him reappear very far off, in the middle of the gully, next to another round head.

Doon Lough. This humbly melancholy corner of the countryside, this pond bordered with yellow irises, which looks as though it is in some corner of the Lorraine plateau. The two swans drifting slowly, followed by five little ones. All that two steps from the tragedy being played out on the rocks and from which the ground echoes with dull thuds.

When I come back, around 3 o'clock, I notice the metal sheet lying on the ground, the door open. Inside, a human upheaval. They have come back shaken, wet, having had to go by Duvillaun, having spent two hours on the crossing. Pat 'was afraid of the sea', but will come tomorrow ... In his place, a third Seán,[43] the one who brought us to the island last autumn.

The sea, grey this evening under a grey sky, and all in motion. But on the rocks, from having been stirred up again and again, it is no more than melting emerald boiling with big white bubbles.

Six seals in the gully, playing hide and seek. A sign that the gale is going to pick up again.[44]

The three lads had left to pull up some lobster pots, no doubt set down by their friends last Saturday. On the shore, behind the Bailey Mór, we can see the currach. We go down to it. The wind is turning to the south. They had every sort of difficulty rounding the tip of the island. They unload the lobster pots, and after lifting a few others, will put the currach back here in shelter. Five big blue lobsters at the bottom of the currach. One of them walks backwards under the bench. All three of the lads get back down, and, pushing the currach into an eddy, with great thrusts of the gaff they steer clear of a rock they want to avoid and then push off. Finally afloat again, they dance terribly.

❧ 25 June ❧

We were gathering wood on the shore, Ann and I, the men having gone for the weekend – wood, fishing-net floats and glass balls. Two figures appear at the top of the hill: the two little girls from the south island, who have come to spend the weekend with us.[45] They almost step on a young gull, a week old, a bundle of silver and black down, crouching on the ground.

Maggie gathers it up and her nose twitches like that of a young rabbit.[46] She stows it in the lining of her coat. The gull, wild like all those of its species,

---

43 Possibly referring to John (Seán) Lavelle, seen in the photograph with the swan (fig. 20).   44 In the manuscript, the word '*l'orage*' was replaced by '*la tempête*' (both translated in English by 'storm', but the second one suggests winds without thunder and lightning).   45 See p. 73, n. 34. It is unclear how the girls got to the north island. Their father, according to this account, had left to fish on Thursday and this entry is for Saturday so he had not just dropped them on his way out. Local residents tell me one can swim between the two islands, but it seems unlikely the two girls would either have been alone for two nights or left to make their way alone. Perhaps they stayed in another inhabited house on the north island until Saturday.   46 It was common to adopt baby gulls as short-term pets on the island.

47 Ann holding Dick,
the little pet gull.

opens wide and closes its long black beak, looks about furiously and tries to bite without strength. Maggie, unflappable, closes over her coat where the bundle of down cowers, terrified. We go back along the shore. The wind has carried onto the sand whatever the storm has washed up: small pieces of planks, cleats from currachs, bits of *giúsach*, heather from Achill,[47] and a branch, a branch with its bark, come from where? From what faraway wood to this treeless coast? Ann piles them into a potato sack, with cries of delight. The girls trot here and there, gathering, commenting on their finds.

In the evening, we go back. The gull is placed in a basket filled with straw and covered with a lobster pot that has seen better days: Willy Mór,[48] John Joe[49] and the monkey[50] arrive for the evening. W[illy] M[ór] takes his place in the corner by the hearth, very sure of himself. J[ohn] J[oe] sits down beside one of our 'tables', and Maggie, moving like a cat, perches beside him. The monkey is seated on our heap of wood, his knees up with his forearms resting on them, his face screwed up. E[ileen] seizes my painter's stool. I have the whalebone stool, the new addition to our furniture, found by A[nn] in an

---

47 The fishermen of the Inishkeas used to make lobster-pots from Achill heather (see colour pl. 7).
48 Willy Sally Ó Maoineacháin. 49 Séan Ó Cráithín (Creane). These three are the fishermen living in a nearby house on Inishkea North. 50 Henry consistently calls someone 'the monkey' and, while it is not entirely clear whom she means, it seems to be an affectionate nickname she uses to help herself identify one among this group of similar men.

48 Men carrying a currach next to one stored on stone supports.

abandoned house. A[nn] and W[illy] lead the rather hilarious conversation of anecdotes and malicious gossip, sometimes coarse, sometimes childish, which A[nn] punctuates with pantomimes and sketches in which she strides around the room, imitating the posture, the voice, the gestures of Pat Bhán or some other notorious whipping boy of the village. E[ileen] laughs, while maintaining some of her dignity. M[aggie] tries clumsily to lead on J[ohn] J[oe] who, from time to time, gives her a furtive look. The monkey makes a satisfied face. W[illy] M[ór] answers each story with an even more outrageous story. He was in America for a long time, and also in the naval shipyards of Glasgow. Acts the freethinker regarding the *taïvche*. Around midnight the three men get up.

The little girls' father and Philip went out to fish last Thursday, and have still not come back. They do not seem excessively concerned about it.

✾ 26 June ✾

Rainy day. Quite lazy. The girls do not talk much. Ann has a toothache. We lunch on dried peas and potatoes. Ann keeps on hiding the bacon in the bedroom where the lads sleep – where they find it, naturally, rolled up in her coat or her stockings, and fry it as soon as she has her back turned – with the result that we have only a tiny bit left.

During lunch, great commotion. E[ileen] catches sight, far away, off the jetty of Port Tragh [Port of the Beach], of a barely distinct dot, which she says is a currach. A[nn] declares that it is Steph[an] and the three priests, and rushes us to be finished for their arrival. E[ileen], between mouthfuls, looks out for the little black dot, which appears and disappears between the waves. Fog descends on the sea. When it retreats, E[ileen] lets out a shout of triumph: The currach is going to the other island, it's my father coming back! And she rushes off into the rain towards the *Teampull* to get a better view.

The girls and I decide to go out. We come back drenched in a lukewarm drizzle that the wind blows in your face so horiz[ontally] that it carries a little sea-spray to you. From between two houses, Philip's tousled head appears.

He and the father have just arrived to collect the girls. Great commotion. They had not intended to go back before tomorrow morning.

We come back to find two lobsters boiling in the pot. Philip calmly breaks one of the claws and offers half its contents to the young gull, who promptly gulps it down. Lobster – almost as common for them as rabbit is for us. The father arrives, his hands behind his back, more like a schoolboy than ever. Tea, bread and butter with jam and lobster are gulped down, all together. Then the whole band slips away.

The little gull trotting around the house, looking like an overgrown chick with a vulture's head. He runs up to an obstacle, very fast, then stops dead, his beak out in front, wavering a little on his feet.

Old currachs, that were abandoned when people left the island, have been carefully turned over and raised up on supports. One belongs to S[eán] Muirnachan, who had it from his father, and seems to have kept it, for purely sentimental reasons, right next to the house. While the men are gone, Ann calls me: Come and get wood from the currach. We break off pieces from the prow, wherever the wood is exposed, and we make a big fire in which the tar boils and smokes.

That evening, at her comment that we have nothing left to burn, Pat remarks: There are always the currachs. At which, looking very interested, she asks: Do you think we can take wood from them? – Why not, they're no use anymore!

❧ 27 June ❧

A storm ten times more violent than last week. The terrifying force of the wind that scours the land, scrapes the sea, slams against the house, slams and slams, tirelessly, hurling, in furious gusts, now great spurts of rain, now sand that enters through the broken windows, through the splits in the door, seeping in everywhere, making the air suffocating. This pitiless fury, with no majesty like that of the sea, only brutal, relentless, telling of anguish and horror. Tried to go and work at the Bailey Mór. Almost impossible to keep upright. As soon as one enters the dunes, the sand, like a hail of needles.

Dick, the gull, a little less wild. Walks around the kitchen looking like a bitter, prudish old woman with a boa around her neck and her shoulders hunched up to protect herself against the cold. Not very steady on his webbed feet with no heels, and, when he stops walking in hurried steps, he generally has a moment of instability during which he looks at you pitiably.

In the morning, Ann having left the door open, he takes advantage of it to rush off as fast as his legs will carry him. We look for him everywhere. Cannot be found. Ann assures me that he will come back. I am sceptical. He is still so terrified by us that he must prefer anything – even this hellish wind and rain – to our company.

The fishermen, naturally, cannot go out in such weather. At first, they had a certain tendency to exploit us. Now, we seem so much a part of the island that the age-old communism of the countryside is becoming established.

They had tea with us yesterday evening. This morning I am woken by loud hammer-blows. It is the two Willies fixing the hinge that had come off our door, and putting on a latch which they made during the morning. They have no more bread. And Willie Mór, while in America, had got used to living on more than bread and tea.

He brings us a salted fish, then all three come to eat it, dressed with our potatoes. Ann has baked bread for them that they take away with care.

Two hours later they reappear with two large beams, a saw, an axe and beaming smiles. They vie with each other in chopping and sawing; the kitchen fills with shavings and sawdust, but we have enough wood for two days. At the same time, W[illie] M[ór] brings me a strange object that he has found on the sand: a long glass tube in which I recognize one of those bulbs for indirect lighting. From what transatlantic luxury liner did it fall, thrown overboard by a steward annoyed at having to replace the bulbs?

49 Dick out on his own.

The men sit down to enjoy the fire they have made for us. All of a sudden, one of them points to the open door: the gull! It is Dick, perplexed, his beak a little askew. Ann rushes over, apron and hair flying, catches him, and brings him back protesting and struggling. No longer this morning's bundle of down at all. His hard little quills, his blue skin coming through everywhere under something slimy and sticky. He seems very cramped, bony and more like a vulture than ever. He allows himself to be fed voraciously. He even lets himself be held in front of the fire on two open hands, without struggling. He is so voracious that he swallows a huge piece of bread, which sticks half-way down his gullet, giving him a huge goitre. He tries, looking like a suffocating ostrich, to gulp it down. Finally, he notices a basin full of water, climbs up to it and with a loud plop! flops into it with delight to drink, drink, drink. He takes a little water, then carefully lets it run down his throat, his head in the air, his beak pointing towards the ceiling.

✆ 28 June ✆

Rain, rain. The roar of the wind, this rumbling of a frantic boiler, and the lashing of rain on the roof, its sad sound of bells on the windows. Ann has neuralgia and is in a bad mood because we will soon be short of cigarettes. A peculiar person, Ann, who lives in the most indescribable mess without noticing. The other day, she said to me: I want the house to look well if Máire and St[ephan] come.[51] But she was happy enough with pushing everything into the corners, giving it a quick sweep and spreading sand on the ground. I never saw an act or word of goodwill from her as long as I have known her. When she gives herself an air of generosity, it is with other people's goods and because she expects something in return. But she was saying to me just now: if the men come, above all don't give them any cigarettes. Forty years old and unmarried in a place like this, rather surprising. There seems to have been some story, when after having really led him on, she turned down a man who, in her view, did not have enough money. That hard crease in her mouth. The total lack of foresight in this country. When there is wood, when there is food, they don't skimp, and when I remark that tomorrow we may be short: Oh! The weather will surely be good tomorrow.

We walk around the shore looking for wood; we ran out of turf two days ago and we have not an ounce of wood left. But the sea is high – astonishingly high, so much so that the two Willies' currach, in the Drak gully, has its nose in the water, and the terns' nests, in the sand, are flooded. Four pieces of cork, a plank and the few bits of wood that I had put aside at the Bailey Mór, it isn't much. Ann coolly puts it all in the fireplace. Centuries of peasant thrift rise up within me, indignant. Just as coolly, I take it all back out, except for a few shavings that are enough to boil the water. Ann almost weeps. In response to my question: With what will you cook lunch tomorrow, she moans: Pat will come for sure. – And if he doesn't come? – Oh! He'll surely come. – But I glance at the Willies' chimney, there, further down. Clouds of smoke are escaping from it. Ann, in desperation, says: Let's spend the evening with the men since they have a fire. We run down, surrounded by swirling glacial wind. At the sound of our footsteps the door opens, and the figure of John Joe appears. We rush in through the door, which slams in a darkened kitchen, cluttered with lobster pots. In the bedroom, W[illie] M[ór] is warming his feet by a blazing fire; the room is small, with two canopied four-poster beds,[52] end to end, taking up a whole wall opposite the fireplace. One of the beds is full of French lobster pots [*pota franncach*],[53] like a tangle of squirrel cages.

---

51 Referring to Mary and Stephen Keane, in whose house Françoise Henry stayed at Fallmore. 52 The islanders' beds often had canopies, as protection against draughts, dirt and leaking roofs. The canopy was made of wood or fabric. An old sail could do as a canopy or serve as side curtains to retain warmth. 53 According to staff in the Aughleam Heritage Centre, French lobster pots (see colour pl. 6) were those

50 Men rowing a currach filled with French lobster pots.

W[illie] B[eag],[54] very small, quaint and wizened, is stretched out on the red wool felt counterpane that covers the other bed.

We sit down on some crates. W[illie] pushes a piece of mast into the fire. The conversation is as usual with W[illie], memories of travelling, trans-atlantic journeys, and so on. Ann, calmed down by the blazing fire, lets herself be teased.

∽ 29 June ∼

Still stormy, but the sun has come out again, and Achill emerges from the fog, as if washed, bright. All in pale greys with light strokes of gold.

J[ohn] J[oe] leaves around mid-day for the 'mainland'. His currach dances terribly. All during lunch, the geese lift off between each mouthful to follow

introduced to the local fishermen by French merchants for export to France. They were made of bent wood and were better than the type made of Achill heather for catching the larger red crayfish (Fr: *homard*) that the French preferred over the smaller dark blue ones (Fr: *langoustine*). Maurice O'Sullivan, however, in his autobiographical book about growing up in the Blasket Islands, published in English as *Twenty years a-growing* (New York, 1933), pp 187–8, credits English fishermen with showing the local Blasket men crayfish and the use of such pots.   **54** Willy Maria Cawley.

51 Ann in house next to pieces of wood awaiting fire.

him. The W[illies] have gone, forgetting to leave us wood. A[nn] finds a little, but very damp, and lunch is not cooked without difficulties. Ann, hopelessly optimistic, has not given up on Pat. As for me, I hardly expect him in such weather. Dick dies during the morning, from having been force-fed bread, I think.

But nothing lasts before the dreaming sun, the sea once more blue and silver, and the big broken clouds that float on the bay. We leave in the afternoon to make our usual rounds. First we go to see a stone slab that A[nn] found at the Killeen.[55] Then we climb to the summit of the island across fields. The grass all green again, velvety, and a profusion of irises in the ditches. All of a sudden, jumping onto a bank, I see this most precious of things: a piece of wood! An old worm-eaten picket with a little rusty barbed

55 It is unclear how Henry is using this word. She may be applying the local designation for the cemetery as a 'killeen' that could have either meant a place where unbaptized children were buried or where unknown bodies that washed ashore were interred. Since this is the only modern cemetery on the island, however, such usage could only be in a section of the larger plot. Alternatively, she may have known that there are the remains of a much older church in the same burial precinct and used 'killeen' for *cillín*, a small church. Finally, we know one of the cross-slabs she identified on Inishkea North came from the path leading to a later church of St Columkille, which she elsewhere calls the 'oratory' or *'teampull'*, thus also fitting identification as a small church, or *cillín*.

52 Man, perhaps Willie or Pat Reilly, with mast found on island for use in fireplace.

53 Masts washed up on shore near Port Tragh (photograph by Janet Marquardt, June 2011).

wire wound around it. But it's wood! With a cry of victory, I pull on it and it gives, almost dumping me in the ditch. Ann tackles another, while I laboriously pull out a third, enormous this one. One or two more, here and there. But all this old wood is terribly heavy. Suddenly I notice, outlined against the sky, the fantastic architecture of lobster pots passing on the other side of a low wall. I shout, I call, and the two Willies and their donkeys stop. We arrive, carrying our treasure, which we carefully place between two lobster pots.

When we get back, we find a heap of very neat, well cut wood at our door. A[nn], who is beginning to suspect that my attempts at thrift might have a point, makes of her own accord a very small fire under the kettle, remarking humbly: It's a warm evening. We heap our pickets on either side of the hearth, as they are in great need of drying. The fireplace looks as though it belongs in a lumberjack's camp. W[illie] arrives carrying a big section of mast, and sits down, clearly to stay for the evening. All the unwritten local laws of politeness dictate that we immediately make a monster fire with the mast and two of our pickets, and that every five minutes we praise the resulting blazing fire – which really is splendid. As time passes, A[nn] steadily loses the hope – to which she had still clung – of seeing P[at] arrive. She is down to her last cigarettes and is already considering 'borrowing' the only pipe in our colony, which belongs, I think, to W[illie] B[eag]. With Pat's prolonged absence and the storm starting up again, she finally comes to her senses, and no sooner has W[illie] gone than she douses what remains of our logs before going to bed. Her invective directed at P[at] becomes thoroughly picturesque.

✦ 30 June ✦

A strange change of mind in Ann. Obscure grudges, no doubt: an irrational fury at the men who, with all the odds against them, have not brought her cigarettes. A kind of reverence for me, who spoke up – and happened to be right. Until now, I was the stranger whom, together with her people, she considered it rather her duty to exploit. Now there is a kind of unspoken pact between us – the two of us against the men.

Around 1 o'clock, she notices the currach. There is then a general commotion in the house. The aim is to convince Pat that we have no more than a small piece of wood and almost nothing left to eat. She douses the logs, and hides them in a corner of my bedroom. Then she heaps up next to them almost all our provisions, and when Pat and the lads arrive, it's to a bare, miserable room, where no tea and plenty of imprecations greet them.

54 Currach rowed by two men with woman as passenger – the usual arrangement.

๛ 1 July ๛

A[nn] really is wild. She is indignant with the men who, on the pretext of having to go to get provisions, granted themselves a half-day's holiday. She decides of her own accord not to come looking for us until 7 o'clock (and as she has in her possession the only clock that we own ...). For my part, my quiet rage has not abated. I comment on their apathy to the two S[eán]s, who, for all their impish manner, are no less violent for it. After all, I work as much as they do, and more, and I feel I have the right to speak up. I let it be known to P[at] that his way of not returning when a currach came on Sunday, and another went back on Wednesday, doesn't please me, and that I have no time for his constant fits of the jitters.

That evening, I ask the S[eán]s to float the currach for me, saying that I want to go to the south island. S[eán], quite humbly, and somewhat as an apology, says: We will take you. – But that's not what I want at all. I just want to row and I care very little about the south island. In the end, S[eán] and I row. He tries a little to put one over on me, and I pour all my energy into preventing him (those damned round oars that spin in your hand). By chance,

55 Donkeys grazing on the north island.

I do quite well. Enough to justify a dialogue: S[eán]ín: Do you think she could row the small currach on her own? – S[eán]: Yes, certainly. – Strangely, this establishes what I had wanted: a kind of camaraderie which did not exist until now. We climb to the top of the hill. S[eán]ín has disappeared in search of the herd. In the light of the setting sun, the animals appear, having moved among the desert of rocks towards the grassy hill. Five big unpredictable donkeys and the gruff little donkey – still taller than he is long, walking in front.

The joy of the journey back, level with the water, the mountains floating beyond the constantly changing waves, breaking into white horses.

In the evening, Pat is grumpy and moaning. He complains that the bread is too hard. A[nn] very sensibly – for once – having given us first the bread sent by W[illie] M[ór]. The three men are seated outside the door. A[nn] and I inside. In the worst Irish that was ever spoken, I give them a piece of my mind. Bread too hard? And do they think that the people in Dublin have fresh bread every morning, and bacon whenever they want, and how would it be if they were in Scotland? I have had enough of their behaving like spoilt children. I work as hard as they do and don't eat eggs or bacon, and so on. Everything I have on my mind – and other resentments that they couldn't know about – pour out in a rush. (M[aureen] who would not be capable of living the hard life on a farm, or of doing a day's work with a spade, thinking she can lecture me on the lot of the 'workers', the 'poor' and so on.) Total and complete silence on the other side of the door. Probably astonishment, and then this almost too humble way the people here have of recognizing an obvious truth, when it is put in front of them, that they were unable to see. A[nn], who feels that she has been vindicated, is triumphant. She doesn't see more in the exchange than the criticism of her 'hard bread'.

ঌ 2 July ঌ

It seems that Pat imagined that we would keep working here all summer. And yet I had announced last week that there was only enough left for a few days' work. But just the same as A[nn]: this optimism that doesn't face up to the facts. I announce today that we will work no more than Monday and Tuesday. Pat very disconcerted. S[eán]ín vaguely unconcerned. S[eán] visibly disappointed. Life must be hard in the R[eilly] household and while P[at]'s inconceivable laziness is probably the cause, the consequences weigh heavily on S[eán]. An odd boy, S[eán], he would be strangely likeable if one managed to get to know him. Sometimes distant – one would almost say bitter – probably through pure shyness, sometimes, on the contrary, very friendly and talkative. When we are working together, he never runs out of questions about France and how this or that is done there. His curiosity wins out over his shyness at such times. A tall boy, but not strong, less so than S[eán]ín who appears skinnier. Fed almost exclusively on bread and tea, according to A[nn], while in S[eán]ín's family, where there is the drowned father's allowance,[56] and probably a more resourceful mother, they eat well. S[eán]ín and his three brothers always playing tricks. Two are extraordinarily good-l[ooking], with tousled hair, blue eyes sparkling with mischief, and an unexpected regularity in their profiles. Another brother and S[eán]ín have tired-looking faces, with an expressive elasticity, younger versions of their uncle, the captain. Their berets look hilarious. S[eán]ín's was perhaps blue originally. But navy? Or sky blue? Grey would be closer to its colour now. He gives it the shape of a cap, or sits it on his forehead like a question mark, sometimes pulls it back or over his eyes, depending on the mood of the moment. Endless tricks, often at A[nn]'s expense.

---

56 The allowance referred to here for Seánín's mother after his father's drowning in 1927 must have been from the state.

56 Woman in black mackintosh.

A[nn]'s sudden changes of mind!! She had told me that this time the men would surely not go to the mainland, for fear of failing several more times – and that indeed she would stop them. This afternoon, it is they who do not want to hear any talk of going, saying that the weather is uncertain, that there was a seal on the shore of the B[ailey] Mór, a sign of bad weather, and so on, and it is she who says, over and over again, that we are going to go. She adopts a sentimental air to say to me: Wouldn't it be lovely to go to Mass tomorrow morning? What can possibly be at the bottom of this?

S[eán Mac] Faidín's boat is in the port of the south island, taking scrap iron from the Norwegian whalers' camp.[57] A[nn] comes early to fetch us, knowing that I have letters to send. P[at] suddenly says: I'm going to go back on

---

57 This is John Padden; see p. 60, n. 4 on the name. The whaling station was established in 1908 on Rusheen islet. It was a complex operation beset by problems and eventually failed, closing in 1914. For more information, see Rita Nolan, *Life on the Mullet*.

S[eán]'s boat – and adds: I'll send you another of my sons, a good little lad, you'll see, and as strong as I am. I don't give a damn what he sends me, he could send me a monkey and I wouldn't mind, so long as I were rid of him. He is slightly astonished, I think, that I am not clinging to him. We see him aboard, without the sarcastic remarks of the captain, to whom A[nn] gave a colourful account of the situation. The lads, sensing good weather, want to go fishing. They drop us off on our island, run to the house to fetch their lines, and go out again, slim silhouettes in blue jerseys, running in the wind.

A[nn], childish and exuberant, brings me on a walk around the island. I am delighted by the dreamy view, perhaps of Dugort,[58] delighted to have my black mackintosh, and above all delighted to be rid of P[at]. The P[at] stories, which she will keep trotting out indefinitely, later on. P[at], grumbling about the bacon being too salty or the bread too hard, me and P[at]'s *báinín* – and so on. All in friendly exuberance. A different person, whimsical and amusing. She tells me that there must be a pilgrimage to Fallmore tomorrow, with 'lots of cars and people who will come from afar, and the blessing being given to the ruined church in the cemetery', and if the lads catch some fish, they will go to sell it tomorrow, and we shall go with them, and so on and so forth. So that explains her hurry to go to the mainland yesterday evening!!

Around midnight, the lads have not come back and the wind is getting stronger. I go to bed. A[nn] puts her bed by the fireside and prepares the kettle for their return, and a supply of wood to warm them.

During the night, I hear voices, S[eán]ín's excited voice, and imagine his expressive gesticulations. I go back to sleep.

In the morning, A[nn] tells me that the lads came back around 3 o'clock with sixty pollocks, and that they left again two hours later to catch the lorry that will take them to sell them in Ballina. The wind gets stronger and stronger. I hardly expect them. And then if there is all this commotion at Fallmore, God knows when they will come back!!

But in the afternoon, the currach reappears. Our two youngsters arrive, followed by a dazed, shaven-headed child, with a stiff fringe like a lampshade on his forehead. They are half dead from sleepiness, but puffed up with pride: they sold their fish for one pound ten shillings. When I congratulate them, S[eán]ín makes a face like a happy monkey, and S[eán] gives a kind of big brotherly smile. A[nn], baiting Peter,[59] the new acquisition, trying to

---

58 Or Doogort, on the north coast of Achill Island, under Slievemore.   59 Peter Reilly (Peadar Ó Reallaigh), whose pay slip has been preserved: 5 July 1938, 10s. for two days' work on the site (IVRLA, FHC, Stones/Sites/Notes relating to the excavations at Inishkea County Mayo, image 21).

57 Peter digging sand out of pit with probably Seán or Seánín standing above next to Henry's wooden wheelbarrow.

convince him that the condensed milk is donkey's milk, that my painter's stool is a bit of wreckage found on the shore, and so on. But she looks embarrassed at my question to S[eán]ín: Did you see the pilgrimage? – I eventually discover that she let herself be fooled by S[eán]ín, who really took her for a ride.

❧ 4 July[60] ❧

A shame that everything wasn't like this from the start! An uninterrupted stream of jokes at the dig, at P[eter]'s expense. He works as best he can, but has inherited his father's obtuse mind. S[eán], very anxious at first that I might take it badly. Visibly relieved when he sees that I laugh at the child's blunders, and give him moments of rest without seeming to. As if by accident, as soon as Pat has gone, the '*cr[ámha] duinne*'[61] appear! S[eán]ín sinks his spade right into a skull – just below the place where P[at] was working on Saturday! I have the broken stone slab placed on the grave, while shuddering at the thought of all the problems that P[at]'s departure has spared us. At eleven o'clock, a song carried by the wind announces the arrival of A[nn], who appears at the top of the wall, her head wrapped in a kerchief with white polka dots. Innocently, she goes straight down to sit on the slab. When it is explained to her where she is, she simply changes the tone of her song, stops unwrapping her pieces of bread and butter, takes her head in both hands and, rocking back and forth, starts to keen at the top of her voice. The cries of the passing gulls answer her rhythmic moans. The lads are half laughing, and P[eter] looks at her with alarm. She weaves fragments of song into the ritual sobs, adapting the words to the '*sean-fhear*' [old man] who rests below her feet, then launches into a song in English about the disaster of the fishermen of Inishkea – without consideration for the fact that among them was S[eán]ín's father. Without any transition, she returns to her normal voice to hand out our cups, moves on to some mischievous story, then at the end pours the remainder of the tea on the grave: Now, there's some for you (addressed to the '*sean-fhear*') and you keep quiet ...

Continual fits of laughter caused by P[eter]'s bustling clumsiness. More talk of the mermaid. Ann says that she has seen her. Seán, who had never spoken of it, confesses: I have often seen her. Seánín, jokingly, asks him: She didn't come out of the water to see you? S[eán]'s gaze vanishes far, far away:

60 For 4 and 5 July, Henry accidentally wrote 4 and 5 June.   61 Variant on *cnámha duinne*, human bones.

No, of course not. S[eánín] continues: All the same, a handsome fellow like you. Seán, distant, with an edge of anger: No, she only comes onto the shore. I know the place.

❧ 5 July ❧

In an ever better mood, tinged with a little sadness that all this is finished. The lads are about to go off fishing at Inishglora.[62] S[eán], with slightly amused astonishment, says to me: You're staying another week? – And longer if I can. – Oh, in the summer, yes. (But despite everything, he admitted to me the other day that perhaps he did regret being in Glosh now. And that he was so happy to have an opportunity to live on the island again.) I say to him: You will come and see us if you fish around here. A face lit up. Ah sure – you will see us before the end of the week.

The transatlantic liner that can be seen gliding over there, very far away, towards Achill. The other day, it was the white sail of the *Samson*.[63] But today, what is it? What can a boat of that size be doing in Blacksod Bay??

They laboriously sign my pay-sheets.[64] P[eter], the most easily, in Irish, then S[eán]ín, then S[eán], kneeling at the table, in English, with excuses for his slowness due to his hands shaking after the work. They bundle up their blankets, take away the big lid, which served as one of our tables, and their lines. They put my letters inside their caps, carefully repeating my instructions. Then, with a little hesitation, they make as if to say goodbye. I protest,

---

62 'Inis Gluaire', an island north of the Inishkeas, almost 3km offshore from Cross Point. St Brendan (or 'Bréanainn of Clonfert'), called 'the Navigator' (*c*.484–*c*.577) and said to have sailed to North America, founded a hermitic monastery there.   63 The *Samson*, a Norwegian seal-hunting ship, was built in 1855. For a long time she fished off Newfoundland. Afterwards, towards the end of the 1920s, the *Samson* was sold to the explorer Richard Byrd, who used her for his first Antarctic expedition in 1926–9. She sank in 1954. Some claim that the *Samson* was near the *Titanic* at the time of her shipwreck on 15 April 1912, but others dispute this claim.   64 Several of these pay sheets have been preserved. For Patrick Reilly on 18 June 1938, £1 17s. 6d. for seven and a half days' work on the site [IVRLA, FHC, Stones/Sites/Notes relating to the excavations at Inishkea County Mayo, image 26], of John Reilly on 5 July 1938, £1 5s. for five days' work, undated receipts for £1 15s. for seven days' work, and £1 10s. for six days' work [images 22, 24, 25 respectively] as well as 5 July 1938 for £1 5s. five days' work by his father [image 23], of Seán Ó Maoineacháin some undated receipts for £1 5s. for five days' work, £1 10s. for six day's work, and £1 15s. for seven days' work [images 23, 18, 19], finally of Seán Ó Craithín on 23 June 1938, 10s. for two days' work [image 17]. Françoise Henry's small ledger also notes, for 15 June, 'Paid wages: £1 10s. Big Seán (6 days) + £1 10s. Little Seán (6 days) + £1 7s. 6. Pat (5 days ½) = £4 7s. 6d.' [image 94] and, dated 18 June, 'Paid wages: 10s. Big Seán (2 days) + 10s. Little Seán (2 days) + 10s. Pat (2 days)' [image 95].

laughing, and we all go down to the boat, one carrying a spade, the other a bundle, and A[nn] carrying nothing. They lift the currach over their heads, taking it down to the sea. S[eán]ín jeers at P[eter] and A[nn]. S[eán], more serious, as if looking for a way to show that he regrets leaving, half stands up in the currach, and without quite turning around, holds out his hand to me: *Slán leat, anois* [Goodbye, now]. The others, clumsily, also shake my hand. S[eán], who is keeping the boat balanced on a wave with his oars held out, while the others jump on the stern one after the other, shouts to us: We'll be back on Sunday! – And then the next wave carries them off.

The fishermen have still not come back. The two of us are alone on the island.

✀ 7 July ✀

Dug up the corpse, on my own, the storm blowing heaps of sand into the hut, this fantastic wind that whistles in the grass and that is stopped by no tree. Lapwings and gulls reeling off shrill cries in the sky, and the yellow bones, the colour of old amber, slowly emerging from the sand under my trowel – brr.

✀ 8 July ✀

J[ohn] J[oe] brings me a letter from L[eask] announcing that pickets have been sent.[65] I need to talk about it to the captain, who is once more on the other island. We go, A[nn] and I, to the tip of the island, she waves a white cloth, I shout at the top of my voice. A moment later, a currach breaks off from the boat, and the captain and one of S[eán]ín's brothers arrive having rowed across, obviously wondering if one of us is in mortal danger …

The two W[illie]s have also come back. We spend the evening in their house. Three men in the shadow of the canopy, W[illie] M[ór], A[nn] and me near the fire. One can see huge hobnailed soles, and the faint outline of J[ohn] J[oe], who puts his hand on his hip like a figure of Giorgione when he speaks to his neighbour.

A[nn] adopted four wild ducklings that she caught in the crook of a little dry stone wall. She bathes, force-feeds and fondles them so much that they

---

65 See the letter of 1 July 1938, addressed to Françoise Henry from Harold Leask, Inspector of Historic Monuments (IVRLA, FHC, Stones/Sites/Notes relating to the excavations at Inishkea County Mayo, images 39–42).

58 Probably Seán (or Seánín) in house on north island with board used to keep door shut against wind and animals, wearing hobnail boots.

die after two days. A young calf comes to expire in the enclosure opposite our door. It takes a whole day to die, and every time one passes, it looks, with a beseeching and half-defeated gaze, at this human who will give it no help ...

❧ 10 July ❧

The fishermen left last night – the Willies with a small sail on their currach, which went off slowly. The two others, rowing – little black dots slowly shrinking in the immensity – come back this evening. A new fellow, in M— Cawley's place,[66] one Seán Pat, about 35 years old, a round, stubborn face, under a protruding cap.

66 Either Michael or Martin Cawley.

59 Men setting posts for barrier around excavations. Some of the men must have come with the shipment for this job, as they are not Henry's regular workers. The three on the left have been identified as Patrick, Seán (Seánín) and Michael Meenaghan, the sons of Seán Michael Meenaghan, the only married man who drowned in 1927 storm (see p. 64, n. 19), while Stephan Keane can be seen in his lighter suit in the group on the right, with a priest coming up from below.

✤ 11 July ✤

Waited all morning for the boat, which did not come. Quite rough weather, but not enough to justify this strike.

Finally, around 1 o'clock, we see it, buffeted between the islands. It drops anchor opposite the Bailey Beg. First the two priests[67] disembark, then Stephan, very stiff and solemn in his Sunday tweed. The younger of the priests is talkative, quite young with a pink, round face set on his white collar. He is very excited to 'come and see the Robinsons[68] on their island'!

67 Named in letter of 19 July 1938 from Mary Keane as Fr Kehoe and Fr MacCarthy (IVRLA, FHC, Stones/Sites/Notes relating to the excavations at Inishkea County Mayo, image 58).   68 The analogy with Daniel Defoe's novel was also used by Maurice O'Sullivan (*Twenty years a-growing*, p. 126). It is also very present in Françoise Henry's mind when she announces her arrival in Inishkea in a letter addressed to Adolf Mahr, director of the NMI, 12 June 1938: 'here I am and I wish you could see us! This has more in common with Robinson Crusoe than any excavation you have ever sponsored' (Archives, NMI, E63: L-L28 Inishkea North).

1946 journal[1]

ᔐ 3 August 1946 ᔑ

Arrived at Louisburgh. Nice little hotel. Bought a few things in some small shops where everything is piled up into an improbably balanced heap. An old fellow says to me: Don't worry: after the 8th there will be good weather. Old Moore says it, he is never wrong![2] And he wraps up one or two things for me in pieces of newspaper, and sees me out with a deliciously inadequate 'safe home'.

ᔐ 4 August ᔑ

Was at Roonah to try to go across to Caher.[3] After lengthy negotiations, I find myself a crew made up of a boy from Connemara, for whom the sea must hold few secrets (he comes from the mouth of Killary Harbour) and a local boy (a 'native', as the Connemara lad says with a certain disdain), very self-important and ignorant. The weather, which had been dazzling all morning, turns leaden. There was a gale the previous night. We all agreed that the sea would calm down minute by minute, but once the currach is out of the port, we are seized by the full force of the waves. I had forgotten what a tiny cork a currach can be under a big, swelling wave. Little by little, the sky grows more and more leaden, then fades into a fine, penetrating rain that seeps through everything. The coast has vanished; Clare Island and the rocks of Mweelan[4] are gradually fading. Nothing remains before us except the long, grey shape of Caher. An old man, this morning, told me of the ghostly processions that

---

1 The fifth notebook, bound in red cardboard, 25.8 by 20.4cm, is also written in black ink, except for one loose page written in pencil. It is held in the UCD archives and the individual pages are available online at http://hdl.handle.net/10151/OB_0001356_AR. 2 *Old Moore's Almanac*, an annual published in Ireland since 1764, containing useful general information on tides, livestock fairs and horse racing, as well as weather forecasts. Not to be confused with its English namesake *Old Moore's Almanack*, whose first issue dates from 1697. 3 Small island north-east of Inishturk Island. Henry had visited the island in June 1939 but her photographs did not turn out well so she returned on 4 August 1946, the visit recorded here, to retake images for her article published the next year: 'The antiquities of Caher Island (Co. Mayo)', *JRSAI*, 77 (1947), 22–38. 4 On Achill.

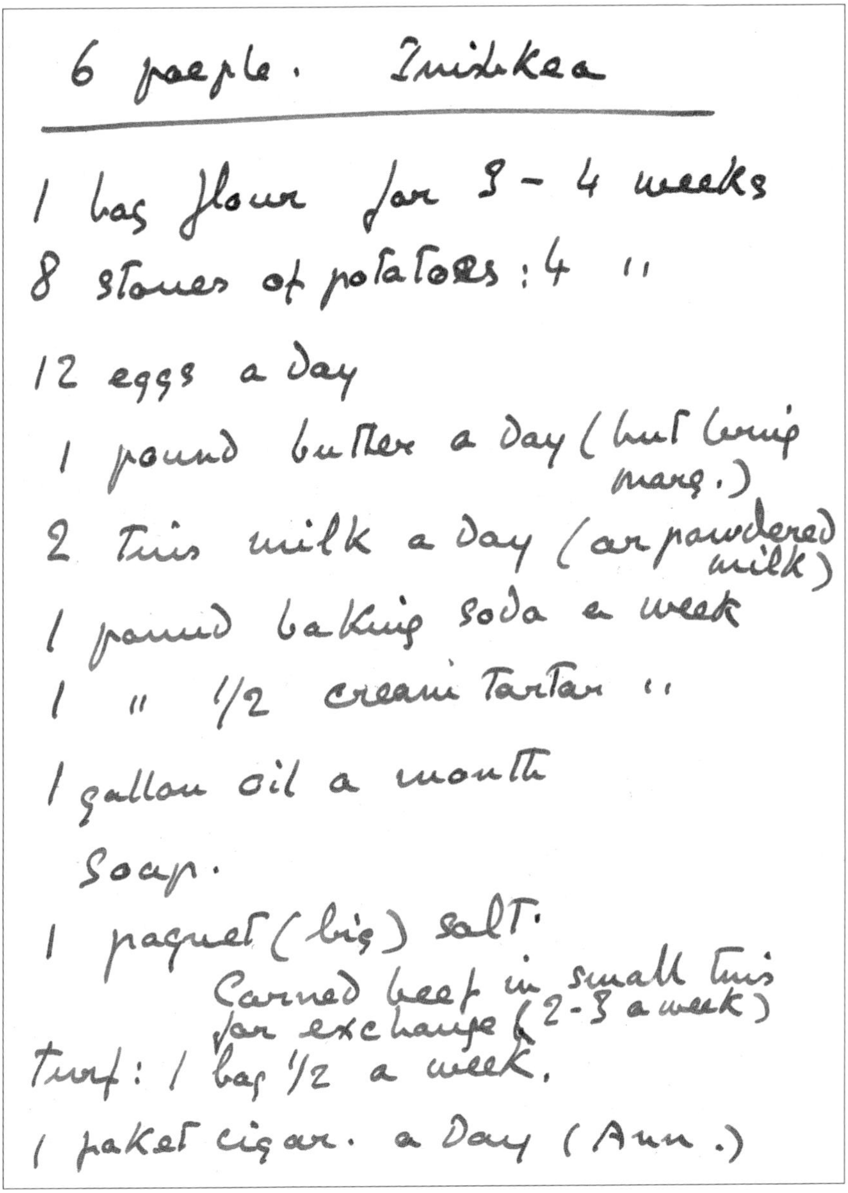

6 people.   Inishkea

---

1 bag flour   for 3 - 4 weeks
8 stones of potatoes : 4 "

12 eggs a day
1 pound butter a day (but lump
                                      marg.)
2 Tins milk a day (ar powdered
                                       milk)
1 pound baking soda a week
1 "   1/2 cream Tartar "

1 gallon oil a month
   Soap.
1 paquet (big) salT.
         Carned beef in small Tins
         for exchange (2-3 a week)
Turf: 1 bag 1/2 a week.
1 paket cigar. a Day (Ann.)

60 Françoise Henry's list estimating the supplies she would need to take to Inishkea
North in 1946 to cover food and fuel needs (from UCD library archives,
FHC: http://hdl.handle.net/10151/OB_0001356_AR).

are sometimes heard saying their rosaries across the island. It is strange for us to be alone in the greyness of this haunted island. In the little bay of Portatemple[5] where we disembark, the big heads of two grey seals appear and disappear; at times, they give this strange impression of standing on tip-toe, and appear out of the water as far as their shoulders, their big round eyes fixed on us. As we disembark, an overly sharp oar stroke by the clumsy one throws us onto the rocks, and makes a badly done repair in the bottom of the currach come unstuck, which lets in some water in small bubbles.

An hour of furious work;[6] the rain stops, happily.

Then we leave again. The fog, a vague and floating fog envelopes us, hiding the island almost as soon as we had left it, hiding everything except the white and blue-green[7] shapes of the waves that form and come apart beneath the boat. – Of course there's fog, says the Connemara lad to the other: you threw stones at the seals; they always send fog to those who annoy them. – They decided to go back with the sail up. I am quite excited, because I have never been in[8] a currach that has a sail. The Connemara boy, who knows the operation by heart, places one oar crosswise, two oars upright to which the sail is attached, and holds it all together with a steady hand.[9] The sail is a piece of a sort of jute canvas in which there are more holes than surface (happily for us, I think). The Simple Simon,[10] steering the currach from the aft with an oar. He constantly lets out exclamations – about how this is the first time he has been at the helm, how the currach rises marvellously on the waves. Then, he makes a move of the tiller that sends us out of the wind, and makes us roll like a bit of cork in a greenish hollow. The other, unflappable, pulls on the right rope, gives it two turns around the cleat, puts us back in the wind, and the tattered rag swells once more, triumphantly.

Great discussion to decide whether we are not, in the fog, going off to America. They get so heated that they end up asking my opinion of the identity of the vague shapes that appear at times in the mist. I am busy, using a battered old steel plate, to bail out the water that rises insidiously in little bubbles through the piece that has come unstuck at my feet. I lift my head, and try to give my opinion without batting an eyelid, even though the comic aspect of my being consulted on a coast which I am seeing from this angle for the second time in my life gives me a strong urge to laugh. All things

---

5 In Caher Island.   6 See p. 106, n. 3; this refers to the photographs Henry took.   7 The author initially wrote 'grey'.   8 The author initially wrote 'never seen a'.   9 A sketch of the sail on the prow of the *currach* appears on the third page of this notebook (fig. 62).   10 Henry used the term *Jocrisse*, a figure of fun in French comedy, made ridiculous by his clumsiness and gullibility.

61 Loose note that Françoise Henry made prior to the 1946 dig on Inishkea North, listing the utensils and tools that Ann Cawley had kept (from UCD library archives, FHC: http://hdl.handle.net/10151/OB_0001356_AR).

considered, and having identified the ghostly capes, we were not going to America, but indeed to Achill ... We complete the crossing by rowing.

ഇ 5 August ∾

Explored a little of the coast. Not as much as I would like. But the wind is raging. Everything becomes exhausting.

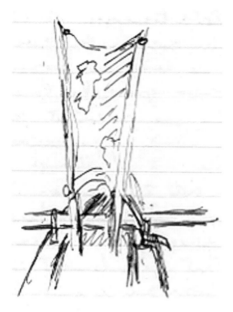

62 Sketch on blank page in Françoise Henry's journal for 4 August 1946 of Connemara boy's makeshift sail for the currach on return trip from Caher Island (from UCD library archives, FHC: http://hdl.handle.net/10151/OB _0001356_AR).

✜ 6 August ✜

Bad weather. Stayed at the hotel and wrote my article, among the comings and goings of cyclists on holiday, and of ruddy-faced English salmon fishers, decked out in faded cardigans and ragged tweeds.

✜ 7 August ✜

Explored to the south of Westport.

✜ 8 August ✜

Typed my article, in a shop, where a rather unreliable typewriter had been made available to me.[11]

---

11 The author added here, in pencil, 'in Westport'.

◆ 9 August ◆

The day fixed for my arrival at Achill Sound. I said that I would like to leave for Inishkea the day after. My ambition seemed comical to me the whole week when the gale blew without stopping. But as day breaks it is almost calm. Was it Old Moore?[12]

Went to see the most impressive carved pillar of a cross, at the edge of a bay, before a great background of mountains. In the slightly calmed air, the countryside becomes immense, with big clouds sculpted in white, dipping blue gaps suddenly open above dark mountains, and shadows, velvety blue, that slide slowly over the endless, stripped peat bogs. Hot sun. Leaving Mulranny, the gorse grains were cracking like pine cones in a fire.[13] Near Kildun, the rhododendrons of a 'shooting lodge' that have become wild, and are growing everywhere the turf has been cut away.

Arrived in Achill in the evening. Welcomed in J[oe] S[weeney]'s name by a friendly little cousin, a slim woman in a black coat. My various parcels seem to have arrived – and to have caused some amusement. We leave making the inventory to the following day. I am promised that we can leave tomorrow, if the weather holds.

◆ 10 August ◆

Distinctly favourable weather. I go out looking for J[oe] S[weeney] in the morning. I am told that he has just gone to meet me. I go back out and finally find him on the bridge. I was expecting a crafty old shopkeeper, and find a bespectacled young man, dressed in the most severe black, seemingly both timid and self-assured – a disconcerting combination. He tells me that it will certainly be possible to leave this afternoon, brings me into the shop and hands me over to one of his employees, who at first wants to give me no more than a few kilos of potatoes, and says to me: But you will come to get some more. When I explain to him that I will be in Inishkea, he responds without batting an eyelid: Oh, in that case, I will give you all that you need now. One has the impression that the shop is accustomed to facing any eventuality. Besides, it is a gigantic shop that has everything, from sunglasses and ceramic dogs to flour and macaroni. Behind, there is a little town of warehouses where some lorries are manoeuvring. Another employee guides me through the

12 See p. 106, n. 2.   **13** Gorse buds 'explode' when they open.

63 Two men carrying supplies down the road to Port Mór at Surgeview.

maze where we find some of my parcels. But I am still missing the wheel-barrow. Suddenly I see it next to a lorry whose load J[oe] S[weeney] checks. He turns back, surprised: That belongs to you? It's a good job you saw it! I was going to send it to the other end of Achill. Affable, but distant, and certainly very absorbed by the complicated divisions of his establishment, very 'merch[ant] king'.

After lunch, I go down to the boat, which is loaded to perfection, and where I find 'Johnnie', the man who knows everything about boats, who says to me: We're off. I say to him that I thought that J[oe] S[weeney] was coming on the boat. He tells me no, he doesn't think so. Affairs of state, clearly. A little nephew is the ship's boy. We leave on a perfectly calm bay. The mountains pass by – distant, washed in the sun, blue and pink to the right – closer, enormous to the left, where Slieve Mór rises little by little. Right at the end of the bay, in the 'Bull's Mouth', there are people gesticulating on a headland. 'Heavens, the boss!' cries Johnny. Yes, still impeccable, dressed in black and perfectly unflappable, it is indeed the m[erchant] k[ing], and a little further on, among the rocks, the little cousin from yesterday evening. Johnnie manoeuvres towards the tip. J[oe] S[weeney], with a few brief words, directs him towards a rock from which he will be able to embark without getting the gleaming polish of his black shoes wet. But the leap, like a cat or porpoise, with which he climbs on board does not match his stiff exterior at all. The little cousin climbs quite well, but he [Sweeney] has the balance that only comes with a familiarity from very early childhood with boats and the sea. He sits down on board, fiddles with the motor, jokes about my luggage (I say to myself: What will it be like at Glosh?) and tells all kinds of stories about sea birds.

At Glosh, the adventure turns epic or burlesque, I am not sure which. We disembark at the jetty half-demolished by a recent gale, and the end of which can now only be reached from the top of the parapet. At the top of the parapet, I meet Ann, carrying a big sack (the hay for her bed), and she throws herself into my arms. She exclaims, throwing her arms up, while I try to keep my balance. Then I meet Annie Gaughan a little further up. Around the little boat, there is much activity, mysterious comings and goings of currachs loaded with the most unlikely things. J[oe] S[weeney], caught between fits of laughter and a modicum of anxiety for his boat, asks me timidly: How many people are we taking on board? I have to admit, shaken myself by a fit of laughter, that I have not the least idea. And truthfully, judging by the way all the little urchins of the country are climbing and hanging on, by their hands and toes, to the edges of the tarpaulin, one might wonder. The O'Dalys[14] arrive, with a priest, staying with Stephan, who turns out to be a friend of J[oe] S[weeney]. Introductions, pleasantries; meanwhile, the most unexpected figures pass in a frieze on the lopsided parapet of the quay. Children in big white woollen jumpers, tousled and wide-eyed, leaping like monkeys, my workers each loaded with a big sack of straw (one of them is old Anthony Muirnacháin, who is 75),[15] then a young man wearing a blue jersey and cap, very tall, who walks in little steps holding a 2- or 3-year-old toddler by one

14 Cearbhall Ó Dálaigh and his wife Máirín (Maureen) (see p. 57, n. 66). Her husband brings her to the Mullet for this 10 August departure and a letter from Stephan and Mary Keane on 1 September indicates that he came back to fetch her when she returned (IVRLA, FHC, Stones/Sites/Notes relating to the excavations at Inishkea County Mayo, image 55). This letter also records the Keanes' regrets that Henry would not be visiting them. Since the house that she rented on the island both times belonged to Joe Sweeney, one assumes that when she contacted him for 1946 he offered to handle supplies and transport directly from Achill. At the end of the 1946 diary, she refers to word from Sweeney about a boat from Achill to take her back there. It does make one wonder, however, if she might have been deliberately avoiding renting a room from the Keanes and using John Padden for the main transport again. 15 Miss Cronin had written to Henry in May of 1946 that it would be hard to find workers after early May as most of the men went to work in England during fair weather. However, on 14 July 1946, Ann Cawley wrote that she was ready to go and had three men (IVRLA, FHC, Stones/Sites/Notes relating to the excavations at Inishkea County Mayo, images 81–2, 87–8). This Anthony Muirnacháin may be referring to Antoine Tommy Ó Maoineacháin, the father of Eileen and Maggie on the south island, who visited Henry 25/26 June 1938 (see p. 59, n. 2 on names).

64 Loading the motorboat at Surgeview. One can perhaps identify the seated figure in black to be Ann, while the younger woman perched on the gunnel could be Maureen or Sweeney's cousin.

65 Loading the motorboat at Surgeview. The famous wheelbarrow is upside down on the piles of supplies. Henry noted on the back of the photograph 'Lavelle kids'.

66 Transferring supplies from motorboat to currach to shore.

hand, while with the other he grips a pair of tongs, doubtless refused by Ann. The loading organized itself. There is a wheelbarrow, its wheel in the air on[16] the tarpaulin, beside a sack of flour and a three-legged pot. The stern is snugly stuffed with bags and parcels of all kinds between which are wedged the three workers, Ann, the cousin, the little ship's boy, Maureen and me. We are towing a currach in which is wedged another wheelbarrow whose bright orange paint shines out beside the gleaming tar. J[oe] S[weeney] and Johnnie take refuge in the hatchway, near the engine.

Swift crossing. The sea thankfully not too rough. The currach dances a little, but follows. The strange cargo in the bow manages not to slide.

Unloading on the beach, by return journeys of the currach. The most implausible array of gypsy luggage when everything is spread out on the sand, beneath two currachs buttressed on the rocks like sleeping seals. The cargo is brought up, its bearers slipping on the sand.

The house is in an indescribable state. Fisherman have camped there; on the floor is a confused mixture of sprouting potatoes, straw, rabbit skins and various fishing devices. There is now a bed built in the kitchen, a strange monument of planks and beams, with four pillars at the four corners, but no

16 The author initially wrote 'upended on'.

67 Close up view of seal on rocks at the Dock (photograph by Sean Lavelle, March 2009).

canopy. There is also a sort of table. In our bedroom, there is a pile of kapok extracted from lifebelts, lobster pots, nets and so on.

Ann manages to create a semblance of order in the kitchen, and in the twinkling of an eye lights the fire, and we sit J[oe] S[weeney], Johnnie, the cousin and the little ship's boy down in front of a well-earned tea. Then they leave with promises to return soon.

Walk around the island with M[aureen]. In the Drak, a big seal's head that splutters and blows like a horse at the top of a hill. He looks at us as calm as you like, dives, reappears closer to us, and starts blowing again at the water's surface. A little black head appears in the seaweed on the other side, a gleaming back follows, and the whole, with plenty of airs, also comes nearer, and sits in the rising tide, like its mother, and starts spluttering and sneezing.

On the shore, all kinds of wreckage, pieces of rafts, triangular water cans, mine detonators, etc.

The lake[17] has been completely invaded by reeds and has almost vanished, inundated with sand during a gale. There are no more swans.

17 Doon Lough.

68 Sheep grazing on north island.

✌ 11 August ✌

Moving in. We manage to move the nets into a corner of our bedroom, the kapok into another corner, and we put ourselves in the two others. Ann finds a lobster tank,[18] which she uses as a sideboard (purely decorative: one cannot put anything in it). She digs out from somewhere the stools made from whale vertebrae, crates of all sizes that serve as varying seats and a second table. Everything is put in its place.

This dying island. The sea gnaws at it, breaking the granite slabs, throwing them back on top of the cliffs, devouring the sand wherever it can reach it. The wind wears it away, little by little removing the dunes. The rabbits undermine it. Huge rabbit warren a little above the lake. But they dig everywhere, exposing the roots of the grass with these little beginnings of holes that they dig wildly wherever they can, giving a grip to the wind, to the rain. The sheep, a great many of which are put here now, gnaw it away.

Almost all the flowers grow level with the ground, with tiny stalks. Ground-hugging scabious, low-spreading umbels, gentians that scarcely break the surface. Everywhere there is a little bright pink flower, a bunch of little stars mounted on roots.

18 The author initially wrote 'lobster pot'.

69 'Little ruffled daisies … infinitely soft between sharp rocks'
(photograph by Janet Marquardt, June 2011).

Was at the port. There, not reached by the sheep, a real 'rock garden'. Little ruffled daisies, bladders of campion, all this fragile, infinitely soft between sharp rocks, above a sinister fissure where the sea swells, and fissured rocks that will soon fall into the chasm.

✠ 12 August ✠

Terrible day of work: a north wind that makes the sand stick in our eyes. The sand is made of minute bits of shells, sharp like needles …

✠ 13 August ✠

More entertainment: the rain. We have to stop working around 5 o'clock. But this morning I found, as I went into the kitchen, five big fish spread on the floor. 'A present', says Ann, with a satisfied look. In answer to my questions, she explains: 'It's the man who stopped you taking the stone slabs, the last time.[19] He was dying of embarrassment, and sends you that ...'. Few gifts could satisfy me – and reassure me – as much. After tea, the three men disappear, clearly led off by 'the captain', that is to say old Anthony. An hour later they return, drenched and beaming, carrying driftwood that they leave on the ground, noisily: We've worked well, says the captain, to point out, without insisting, that they wanted to thank me for not having let them work in the rain. The atmosphere has certainly changed in the last eight years.

❧ 14 August ❧

Perfect day. Sun, a gentle breeze, the sea absolutely blue, intense, saturated, under a great pale, light sky where some clouds rest. The granite of Achill's cliffs shines in the sun.

❧ 21 August ❧

Worked with Maureen at House H,[20] which is on the south slope of the Bailey Mór. Around the middle of the afternoon, we notice a big black spot moving somewhere between Duvillaun Mór and D[uvillaun] Beg. A boat coming from Achill, clearly. We recalled all the passages of St Col[umba][21] on 'a troublesome guest',[22] and lose ourselves in gloomy conjectures, imagining the most painful incursions, seasick visitors who will insist on staying, and so on. Meanwhile, the boat takes shape little by little. A mast can be made out. Our men, whom we consult, soon decide that it can only be J[oe] Sw[eeney]'s trawler – but with whom on board?? The boat grows larger. Its black hull and the fine line of its mast suddenly give the measure of the immense landscape, and the blue and gold cliffs seem to grow bigger, the sea seems to spread further into infinity. Just as we are anxiously preparing ourselves to go and

19 John Sibby Reilly. 20 For 'House H', see Françoise Henry, 'Remains of the Early Christian period on Inishkea North, Co. Mayo', *JRSAI*, 75 (1945), 140 (Pindar anthology, vol. 3, p. 214). 21 *Life of Saint Columba, founder of Hy., written by Adamnan, ninth abbot of that monastery*, ed. William Reeves (Edinburgh, 1874). 22 Reference to ch. xxi of the *Life of Saint Columba*, entitled 'Of another man in distress who was crying across the same sound'. 'On another day, the saint heard some person shouting across the sound, and spoke on this wise, "that man who is shouting is much to be pitied, for he is coming here to ask us some cure for the disease of his body; but it were better for him this day to do true penance for his sins, for at the close of this week he shall die". These words those who were present told to the unhappy man when he arrived. But he gave no heed to them when he had received what he asked, and quickly departed, yet before the end of the same week he died, according to the prediction of the saint'.

70 Outline of a 'house' in excavations.

welcome the hypothetical guests, the motor stops, the boat begins drifting slowly, and soon it becomes obvious that it is simply fishing. For two hours it stays like that, moving before the island, little by little, a close and unattainable presence, a black ink drawing on the broken sea.

❧ 15 August ❧

Father Murphy visits.[23] He brings newspapers, letters, all incongruous things on the Bailey Mór. Apart from that, he fits quite well with the place. After having visited the ruins, he sits down on a stone and watches us dig, scratch and sift. Meanwhile, Ann must have been really busy. When we arrive, the area around the house is almost clean, sprinkled with sand, and she, wearing her nicest dress, comes to the doorway to do the honours.

❧ 16 August ❧

Michael Henry visits.[24] If it goes on like this, how will we ever get any work done!

23 This possibly refers to a priest staying with Stephan Keane.   24 This is Mícheál Mac Énrí, a retired

71 Annie Gaughan, Stephan Keane, and unidentified priest outside 'Sweeney House' on Inishkea North.

Read the life of St Columba to Maureen ... 'by the arrival of a certain troublesome guest'. And also, 'The man who is shouting beyond the strait is not a man of refined sentiment, for today he will upset and spill my ink-horn'.[25]

✎ 22 August ✎

The usual complications with Ann. The eggs disappear as if by magic. I am reduced to counting them each morning, and acting fierce if there are more missing than is reasonable. But just when one feels ready to beat Ann, one can

schoolteacher, recruited by the Folklore Commission (founded in 1935) to collect stories, prayers and records of all kinds in Irish, to bear witness to a vanishing world. He collected lore and traditional craft descriptions from the Inishkea families on the Mullet Peninsula in the 1950s, many of whom are mentioned in Françoise Henry's diaries. An article about him by Crístóir Mac Cárthaigh entitled '... and a wooden peg from which emerged a rope ...' is forthcoming in a yet unnamed anthology to be published by UCD Press. See also letter of 17 June 1946 (IVRLA, FHC, Stones/Sites/Notes relating to the excavations at Inishkea County Mayo, image 86).   **25** Reference to ch. xix of the *Life of Saint Columba*, entitled 'Of the inkhorn, awkwardly spilled'. 'On another day a shout was given on the other side of the Sound of the Iouan (Sound of Iona); the saint hearing the shout, as he was sitting in his little hut, which was made of planks, said "The man who is shouting beyond the sound is not of very sharp wit, for when

only burst out laughing because she is really a big baby. I think that the fishermen like eggs ... I am happy to give them some, but at least I would like to know ... That would probably be too simple. There is an unwritten convention by which I give the others a tin of corned beef from time to time to thank them for the fish we are provided with as 'gifts'. It would be simple if Ann would tell me when it would be appropriate to give a tin. No. Instead of that, she makes herself inscrutable, and announces to me at breakfast: the fishermen have no fish. I say, astonished: really? – Ah, I've only asked John Reilly. Maybe Willie brought some back last night, who knows? And she looks, vaguely, through the dirty pane of the window which she stubbornly refuses to clean. I say: If you go to Willie's house, perhaps you could bring him a tin of corned beef? – She livens up slightly: Yes, he'd like that. When she brings us our tea at the Bailey Mór, she whispers triumphantly to me: I have some fish!

The flour was disappearing extraordinarily quickly, and the sack of potatoes remained stationary. I make enquiries about these two phenomena. Ah, you understand, those men don't eat potatoes, so they need lots of bread, she says. – What, they don't eat potatoes? – No, they don't eat them. – Ann, what are you talking about? You will cook them some potatoes. – But I'm telling you that those men don't eat potatoes. – Ann, they will eat them.

She gets up, and, holding her head out in front, goes towards the gable of the house where the three men are talking before going to work. A few minutes later, she comes back, all smiles: I asked them would they eat potatoes if I cooked some today. They said yes, and that they would eat whatever you decide, and they would do whatever you want.

✎ 24 August ✎

The black clouds trail showers through space. The wind wanders like a gull that glides, then flaps its wings. I go to see if there might not be any driftwood at the end of the channel behind the house. After passing the low wall, I jump when I see a human figure beside the channel. It is Saturday. The fishermen have left. There are only the six of us on the island. I soon recognize good old

---

he is here today he will upset my inkhorn and spill the ink". Diormit, his minister, hearing this, stood a little in front of the door, and waited for the arrival of the troublesome guest, in order to save the inkhorn. But for some cause or other he had soon to leave his place, and after his departure the unwelcome guest arrived; in his eager haste to kiss the saint, he upset the inkhorn with the hem of his garment and spilled the ink'.

72 Possibly 'good old Anthony, leaning on his cane'.

Anthony, leaning on his cane, examining like me the cleft in the rock. He has a crate under his arm. He limps over, and says to me: I found a crate. Maybe it will be of use to you? (I use a lot of cases for the excavations). Knowing that he is quietly collecting a little ration of wood to bring back to his house, I offer to borrow it while we are here. But he says, with his gentle smile, shaking his head: No, take it, I brought it for you. We go back quietly in the calm evening.

✎ 25 August ✎

There must have been a gale somewhere out at sea, which missed us. The sky is clear, with light wisps of cloud, but the purple-blue sea hurls huge green breakers, that swell suddenly, in its assault on the cliffs. The rocks towards the south island disappear in a cloud of foam. The island shakes from the dull blows.

Towards the B[ailey] M[ór], sheltered by the island, all is nearly calm, but from time to time the sea, instead of spreading out on the shore, swells before collapsing in a great white crash.

I dig up the skeleton, keeping an eye out to left and right lest anybody should surprise me at this sacrilegious task. M[aureen] arrives after a moment.

She has just been to see the seals at the Drak. There are three today, two big plump monsters, and a third which came to hear her sing, opening wide its big, round eyes.

Around 3 o'clock we notice John Reilly's currach coming back. That probably means our provisions for the week, maybe letters, news from the mainland.[26]

Our men, a completely different team from last time. Two men from Fallmore, peasants little used to boats, calm, excellent workers, very nice, but with none of the quirks of last year's men.[27] Johnn[ie], who is always laughing, but never speaks. To everything one says to him, he responds with a beatific look.

J[ohn] Reilly – Last winter, we stayed for seventeen days on the island without being able to leave, the gale was so strong. We were afraid that the currach would be destroyed.

– Did you have anything to eat? – Oh yes, we caught[28] rabbits, and we had flour. – Do you know how to make bread? – As well as any woman.

Rubber? One day we had three balls at once from the other island. – And then there was some of everything, petrol, turpentine, whiskey, flour.

Ant[hony]: Yes, I had a whole sack of flour one day. Only the outside was damp.

At Inishbofin,[29] they had a whole boat full of whiskey that was going to Germany.

❧ 28 August, 4am ☙

Raging gale. A solid mass of wind that beats, beats like a huge mallet. I am not too sure about the soundness of the chimney, which has a big crack level with the roof. As for what could happen in a house like the Reillys', whose roof is of rusty corrugated iron with holes in it ...

At the Bailey Mór, the tent has probably torn down part of the hut's wall, and the wheelbarrows must have turned into aeroplanes.

---

26 Some notes appear at the end of the page corresponding to the 21st page of this notebook: 'Came to fish wood and all the rest. – No fishing in winter.'   27 This must be an error. There is no evidence that Henry visited the island or employed men in 1945. It would have been nearly impossible the year that the Second World War ended. We assume she meant 'last time' again.   28 The author wrote initially 'had'. 29 Inishbofin ('Inis Bó Finne', island of the white cow, in Irish), situated off the coast of Connemara, opposite the port of Cleggan. In 664, after his defeat at the synod of Whitby, Colman, abbot of Lindisfarne, left Northumbria with numerous monks and came here to found a new monastery in 668.

73 View of village at Inishkea North with Reilly house in centre.

74 Same view of village in June 2011 showing further erosion
(photograph by Janet Marquardt).

The weather had been calm. The sea much less rough than the last few days. But it was cold, grey, dull. As we are in the time of the high tides, the sea, at low tide, smelled bad. Around the end of the afternoon, a great curtain of rain advancing, hiding Achill, over a purple sea. A little rain, stopping and starting. While[30] we are having tea, we notice the Reillys' currach coming back. At night, the wind rises. Michael and Johnnie go down to the shore to fasten the currach.

No, the tent held, and the wheelbarrows too. I went to see in the morning, by the shore. The wind so strong that one can lean against it like on something solid – but moving, and which sometimes throws you back and sometimes lets you down. On the shore, a gull tries to flutter, letting itself be carried, then struggling to go back. Exhausted, it tries to sit, but its tiny weight is not enough to hold it down, and it has to tread the ground constantly to stay in the same place. The sea is not very rough, skimmed too violently by the wind which only tears little plumes of foam from it.

The sheep pile up against each other in the rocks, and look at you with big, wide eyes. No, sheep, it isn't my fault, this raging. The lambs have the astounded look of kittens seeing snow for the first time.

Impossible to work. The men disappear led by Anthony, and soon come back carrying bits of girders, the house of Pat Yet,[31] who lives in Belmullet and no longer wants it, but which goes piece by piece into our fire, broken by blows with stones, since there are no other tools.

In the afternoon, John Reilly arrives (Dominick[32] is never seen), stuffed into a thick turtleneck jersey of white wool, which his wife knitted for him and of which he is very proud. He sits down beside the fire and starts a long conversation with Anthony and Ann (the two others went to join Dom[inick]), one of those basic conversations, about wells (the second well of the north island, which is so good, though the sea gets in sometimes in winter, the well of the south island, which Ann says is a 'holy well', claimed by Anthony to be an ordinary well ('To think he says that, and me wearing out my knees going around it', says Ann), about fishing, about the fair where the island's livestock will be sold, on 15 September, and stories about Michael

30 The author initially wrote 'in the evening'.   31 The name of Pat Cheit (or Yet) implies the use of the mother's name as an identifying element, 'Cheit' being a variant of 'Cáit' or 'Kate'.   32 Possibly Dominick Sibby Reilly, brother of John Sibby Reilly: in the early days of his marriage, Dominick Reilly, going against the wider tendency, tried to live on Inishkea North, but after two years he abandoned the idea and settled on the mainland. He may have been the man with the pregnant wife and baby that Henry saw on the island in 1937.

75 Ann with men in 'Sweeney House' on north island.

Joseph, and Shauneen who has a shop in Glosh,[33] and Martin Michael Phadín
...

Around the end of the afternoon, was with Maureen as far as the Drak. The wind still to the north, cold, but slightly less brutal, simply intoxicating like a chilled wine. Three seals frolicking beyond the current in the Drak. They make as if to come when we call them, then disappear. The sea foaming on the rocks, but in a short, sharp rage, without volume, because it is constantly pounded by the wind. The birds of prey are on the look-out in this apocalyptic weather. Saw the raven get up from one of the gaps in the rock, and noticed its nest, completely covered in white bones. At the next gap, the sparrowhawk climbs and glides.

We came back to find the three islanders still talking by the fire, Anthony leaning his forehead on his cane, his gentle childish face crinkling with mischief, John, his long legs sheathed in thick brown wool, his big arms with a rough coat of white wool stretched out towards the hearth and on the edge of the bed, and his face with its big simplified features enlivened by all sorts of changing expressions. Our two men come back, and Ann makes tea, and

33 Henry confused names here. It was Michael Joseph [McGinty] who had the shop, a small grocery store, in Glosh. He was called Michael Joseph 'Yaye' after his way of saying 'Yeah', an expression he acquired during a visit to America.

offers it to John, who was expecting nothing else, but refuses energetically with a great sweep of his head towards his right shoulder. But Ann, who knows her protocol by heart, ignores it, and pushes him towards one of the whale vertebrae on which he sits without putting on any more airs.

❦ 29 August ❧

Morning of rain and wind. Afternoon of work in the whipping wind.

The evening, same rhythm, our two half-wits disappear, John Reilly appears with the night, and a long conversation takes place between him and Anthony. Ann is in luck.[34]

❦ 8 September 1946 ❧

Since 1 September, the green plovers have returned in great flocks. Wherever you walk on the 'plateau', you raise a flutter of confetti that spirals upwards, with a plaintive rattle, on slowly flapping wings, only to land a little further away. The small ringed plovers, which were living on the shore, are now in the middle of the island and take off too, like agile little arrows, going to sit on some clods, small grey balls that look sidelong at you.

The gulls, quite still, sitting in groups on the shore like big pigeons, blue and white, and a large black-backed gull sitting all alone, looking distrustful or aloof.

There are others lined up on the rocks of the plateau, that don't fly off unless you are very, very near. They need the wind to their faces and if they are on the grass, they take two or three hurried steps into the wind, which lifts them up, and on which they hardly rise with slowly[35] flapping wings.

The sea is blue, the showers are passing.

❦ Sunday, 8 September ❧

Ann and I alone on the island this weekend once more. All the animals seem to know it and become more familiar.

---

34 In the manuscript, the following page is written in pencil and is a loose sheet inserted in the notebook (this is incorrectly labelled on the IVRLA website).　　35 The author initially wrote 'great'.

76 Wall of a type of 'beehive hut', like where Henry took shelter during rain on 8 September 1946.

Followed the birds all morning. Approached very close to the cormorants, as close as the rising tide allowed.

Showers. Took shelter in the beehive. Going back, noticed the tiny black spot of a boat on the sparkling immensity. From this far away, impossible to know what it is. Returned very quickly in case it was our boat. It grows bigger. Flashes of foam at the prow: is it a boat or a currach? Finally saw the orange sparks of the oars on both sides. But Ann announces that there is another boat off Glosh. I can hardly make out a tiny black dot. At other times, golden. Ann says that it is the cattle *poukaun*,[36] with its sail golden or black depending on how it tacks.

During lunch, John Reilly appears with my bag and some letters, and news. The boat is indeed the cattle boat. But Ted Sweeney[37] had a telephone call from Achill announcing that they would come to get us today or tomorrow, and I have a letter from John Cawley[38] saying today, and one from J[oe] S[weeney], who has just gone to England, saying tomorrow. We shall see. Whatever happens, our parcels are ready, numerous and bizarre.

---

36 The islanders, even after relocating to the peninsula, continued to pasture their sheep, donkeys and cattle on the islands. They took the sheep and donkeys in *currachs* and landed on shore, but the cattle could swim to and from larger boats that could carry more of them. A *poukaun* is a type of larger boat with a sail.　**37** See p. 57, n. 67.　**38** Son of Willie Beag, Willie Maria Cawley.

77 Loading cows on to the *poukaun*.

The cattle boat arrived, with ten men on board, and three children who rush into the ruined houses with shouts. The men go to look for the cattle, and bring back two attached by the muzzle, leading seven or eight others that are prancing along.

The small *poukaun* is at the shore, as close as it can come. The men go into the water, dragging the animal, which pulls back with all its strength. A disorderly scrum along the gunwale follows, with everyone pulling, pushing and shouting, and the object of the exercise, inert and reluctant, disappearing in a whirl of flailing arms. The boat leans a little. A few hoarse shouts. Then with a heavy thud, the animal falls back down inside. A second bullock follows, docile and malleable, and goes to join the first. Those that remain on the shore bellow, lifting their heads to the sky.

Some of the men climb on board, water running off them. Others go back, the water up to their waists. They remove the anchor which was stuck into the sand of the shore, and rejoin the others by the currach that was waiting, half lifted on the seaweed at each jolt of the surf.

The russet sail rises slowly and unfolds on the blue sea, on the sparkling sky, like a great corolla that soon falls back into the usual triangle. And the small black hull rushes off with the wind, followed in the distance by the currach, itself all black too.

78 Ann posing with three of the younger men and island donkeys.

The three children stayed, the boat is returning this evening, and come to have tea with us. One of them cut his finger on a tin of food that was lying in the ruins and comes to be looked after, very serious and instilled with a sense of his own importance. After tea, they run off in a barefoot, winged trot, disappear in a field, from which soon rise indignant brays and yells of joy. Headlong stampede as the donkeys that have not been caught snort around two riders who yell and whip them. While the third child runs all around looking for a mount, and the sheep flee, stumbling on the stones, their wool to the wind, and their black muzzles in the air.

It is indeed John Reilly who had stopped me from taking the slabs last time ...!

1950 journal[1]

ꝥ Thursday, 1 June 1950 ꝥ

Ann has 4 men: Pat Monaghan and his currach, and probably a lot of bother, Willie Lavelle, Pat –, Willie –.[2] Seán Phádin [John Padden] promises the boat for 2 o'cl[ock], cost £8 and will send me the men to Máire's house at 12. Out of the twelve parcels sent to Gallagher in Blacksod, eleven have arrived. The wheelbarrow is missing. Seen Miss Cronin.

Went to Blacksod, saw the unemployment people. Rang up CIE,[3] station etc. in Ballina. They promise to send the w[heel] b[arrow] by bus that same evening.

ꝥ Friday, 2 June ꝥ

All was going too well. At 12, nobody. At 1, nobody. At 1.15 I drive to Ann's house.[4] She swears the men are coming at once with a cart. At 2, appears one man, with no cart; the others are at the pier. I show him the stuff: 1 wh[eel] barr[ow], 1 bag of flour, 1 bag of potatoes, 11 boxes and parcels, and send him for the others. At 2.30, drive down to the strand with the smaller parcels. At furious hooting, a man starts leisurely from the pier. Tells me that they are getting a cart, a donkey, a fleet of donkeys ... etc. I leave him the parcels and a piece of my mind, and drive off to Blacksod.

Boat starts at 3 o'cl[ock] from Blacksod, calls at the pier. The four men, Ann and all the parcels are there and embark in spite of fairly strong sea.

---

1 The sixth and seventh notebooks (standard red school exercise notebooks of the day, 20 by 16cm) concern Henry's archaeological dig on Inishkea North in 1950. They are held in the School of Archaeology at UCD. Unlike previous years, these are written almost entirely in English and seamlessly mix together her excavation notes with her personal observations. Some pages contain lists or hourly accounts for the men's work. We have separated the personal diary accounts from the excavation notes and drawings here in order to round out her archaeological experiences on this island and with this group of people. When her comments continue into detailed archaeological remarks, we have indicated the omission by an ellipsis in square brackets.   2 Pat Riley and Willie Beag Cawley.   3 *Córas Iompair Éireann*, the Irish national transport system.   4 By this time, Henry was driving a Fiat 500 in Ireland.

We land at 5 o'cl[ock], disembark at the Porteen Beg. About 10 o'cl[ock], everything, including the turf is up, and I am emerging more or less from the gypsy encampment stage.

∾ Saturday, 3 June ∾

Gale all night. Spells of driving rain this morning.

Started work only at 10, because of late work last night.

Pateen and Willie Beag on House 1 clearing the corner inside. I don't dare to clear outside yet for fear of collapse ...

At 11.30, weather too bad. We go back to the house. Arranged with the men that they will do extra work in compensation.

∾ Sunday, 4 June ∾

The men go to get the lid of the locker of a wrecked boat which they arrange as a table with two oil cans (from the Drack)[5] and a long plank which we fix as a dresser on the Museum['s] tea chests (from the hoard below Columba's Church).

In French:

Yellow irises everywhere. A little water in the lake, but no swans.

Saturday evening, a swift [*martinet*] comes in several times to the kitchen, perches here and there, lets itself be touched, clings to the wall, tail spread; the tail is flecked with white and, fan-like, serves to maintain his balance. [*Small sketch of the bird is below.*] Almost no sea birds' nests. John Reilly says that they are now beyond the Drack. No sign of the seals.

They tell me that there are beehives ('monks' huts') on Inishkeeragh.[6] I rub about 450 eggs with eggo,[7] leaving some unrubbed. 10 eggs a day. I have about 15 extra.

1 tin of milk a day. I have about 6 extra. Butter, 1 pound does three days. Order 5 pounds next week-end.

---

5 Change of spelling for the 'Drak'.   6 There are two islands called Inishkeeragh (Inis Caorach, Island of the Sheep); one in Co. Donegal and the other in Co. Mayo, just north of the Inishkeas. The latter must be the reference here.   7 This is a product that was used to keep eggs fresh by protecting the shells from air.

By keeping the stores in my room I have kept Ann going straight so far. I have 20lbs of sugar. Probably not enough.

Evening: the wind is falling but the sky all grey, soft, as if rain was coming. [*In French*] Two of the currachs landed this evening.

[...]

ᕤ Sunday, 11 June ᕫ

Slept late. Washing. Painted window in men's rooms: all windows painted inside now. Must get paint for outside.

Whilst painting, suddenly see a strange crowd advancing on us. Feared O[']M[eenaghan] invasion. Turned out to be more local, but no less queer.

Pat Monaghan, born on the other island, very nice, insists on talking Irish, and even on discussing Petain's deeds and misdeeds in Irish with me.[8] Slightly ludicrous. His daughter, Kathleen, lives in Dublin, slacks, lipstick, fake diamond earrings. Insists on talking English, though she must have been brought up in Irish. Her husband, from Dublin, talks no Irish, nice but completely bewildered. Pat's son, breezy and cheerful, talking anything you like with great gusto. We have tea, rather Babel-like. Then they depart for a tour of the island, visit the dig, unaccountably leave the floor of [House] 4 peppered with bits of carrageen:[9] then depart from the strand under the Bailey Beg, their currach passing at a short distance from the shore. My men's currach is moored in the same place. From afar, I see with glee the landing of something cumbersome which must be my wheelbarrow.

Pat Reilly has fainted this morning at Mass. Rather worried about him. 71, I have no right to him, except by declaring his son in his place. But has turned out (after all the bother he gave me twelve years ago!) to be my greatest standby. Obviously very keen on earning some money, and would also be hurt to be told he is too old; besides has a currach, and as much at his ease on the sea as if he were a cormorant. I think I will chance keeping him, trying to make work light for him.

The currachs of the fishermen come back, one by one. Walked with Ann to the Drack and back. Seen a seal near the W[est] mouth of the Drack.

Letters.

---

8 Marshal Philippe Pétain was a French military hero in the First World War. He then became head of the Vichy government, which collaborated with the Germans, during the Second World War.   9 A type of moss seaweed.

79 Loaded wheelbarrow on shore with two unidentified women and a man.

☙ Monday, 12 June ❧

Got my wh[eel]-b[arrow] at the dig. The wooden one, which had broken down on Saturday, mended by Pat and Willie Beag with a hatchet and a knife (also a piece of wood!). Works better than before. At last the evacuation of the sand ceases to be a problem …

As the weather was very hot we stopped for two hours in the middle of the day and worked until 7 o'cl[ock]. So no extra hours.

Some lists were glued in here and offer a glimpse of the kind of supplies Henry found it necessary to take for habitation and excavation on the island. We have not transcribed some of the scribbled notes and dates around the margins of the pages.

Frying pan, saucepans, pot, forks, spoons, knives, plates, mugs, cups, towels, blankets, soap, book, sewing things, scissors, strong knife, cotton wool, mapping paper, small note books, 1 or 2 large notebooks, string, black and white chalk, inch tape (rolling), ink, pencils, match boxes, 1 coat and skirt, 1 skirt, jumpers, 1 blouse, 2 waterproofs, socks, sandals, warm pyjamas, woollies, beret, felt hat, shoes, films, trowels, chemist (see next p.), turf, potatoes – 5 stones, butter – 5 p., flour, ~~milk~~ [*crossed out items we assume were simply those she had assembled first*], eggs, apples, oranges, ~~lemons~~, ~~cabbages~~, ~~leeks~~, ~~carrots~~, ~~turnips~~, ~~tins~~ (~~peas~~, ~~fruit~~), tinned milk, tea – 2 p., sugar – 2 p., ~~jam~~, ~~salt~~, pepper, ~~piece of bacon~~, ~~salted fish~~, ~~baking powder~~, bread soda, candles, matches, cigarettes, brandy, iodine, sticking plaster, quinine, Aspros.[10] [*Another shorter list follows*]

80 Unloading sacks of supplies from motorboat to currach to shore.

♫ Tuesday, 13 June ♫

[...]

No extra work today.

The men brought me another ship locker-door which makes me a table in my room.

After some energetic talk to Ann, and the threat that we would eat the corned beef ourselves if no fish was forthcoming, the supply of fish seems to flow normally.

Will have to find where the green stool has disappeared.

Pat Reilly is looking all right.

10 Brand of aspirin.

Yesterday was boiling hot, with a light E[ast] wind. Blue sea, slight haze, Achill hardly visible, sand blinding; today is bitterly cold with a sweeping N[orth] E[ast] wind, which blows the sand about. Short waves running toward the strand below us.

❧ Wedn[esday], 14 June ❧

[...]

The usual labour trouble: W[illie] Mór declares that the food isn't good enough (through Ann). I tell Ann: if he isn't pleased, he can go away tonight (can? with what boat??!) It all arises from the fish. Also, he is the kind to complain. But as he is on the dole, he is in for a damned lot of trouble if he goes on. I didn't speak about it with him. Safer to let everything go through Ann. It will probably fizz out. Anyway I don't care, as long as the three others stay, and my obviously not caring has caused a bit of a sensation. The remark that they ate better than me as I can't eat eggs was also quite efficient. My God, when I remember the way I fed when I was working in the factory, and working ten hours most days![11]

North wind, with showers, cold. Tonight turning into a gale. The fishing currachs come back in haste, the oars glistening bright orange in a ray of sun.

A plane passed five times, very low. Searching for something? Also seen the Granuaile[12] going into Blacksod Bay and out again.

Willie has caught a rabbit with a trap.

[*Note at angle on bottom of page*] One hour extra to each man.[13]

❧ Sunday, 18 June[14] ❧

Slept very late. Made curtains for the kitchen, Ann's bed etc. Intended to go on the other side of the Drack. But about 3 o'cl[ock], terrific invasion. Men, women and children in a horde. Turns out to be the three schoolmistresses,

11 Henry worked in a munitions factory in London at the beginning of the Second World War.
12 Commissioners of Irish Lights' Aids to Navigation vessel, which patrolled the Irish coast. Named after Grace O'Malley, a legendary pirate queen.   13 These notes about the men's working hours occur often throughout the text on the excavation work.   14 Over the course of these entries, from the beginning in 1937, it seems that no one works on Sundays – Henry herself does tasks in the house or occasionally looks further at something in the dig, but the day appears to have been kept a holiday.

the nurse, Garda King[15] and his wife, and a few unidentified others. They ask me to a picnic in the field above the house. Very nice, but when we go down to the B[ailey] Mór, it appears that the men have been there on their own, have walked all over the floor of 3, partly collapsed the section of the post-hole and the side of the trench in the sheep-pen. After that, I don't lose sight of them one minute.

My men came back whilst they are at the Porteen waiting for their boat. Very slow in coming up. When they arrive, they are followed by the gard[a] who invites himself to tea and cross-questions me in a mixture of Engl[ish] and Irish. Am I working for a French museum? And all these bones lying about, are they human bones? etc. etc. Probably some talk of the men behind all that. The one thing he forgets to [do] is to ask me if I have a licence ... Luckily it has arrived in the post brought by the men. All considered, I shall probably send it to him for inspection next weekend.

✎ Monday, 19 June ✎

[...]

Willie Beag is catching more and more rabbits, some in traps, some caught flying, literally! Have taught Ann how to cook them without making them as hard as leather.

In the afternoon, the men suggest that I might like to go to the S[outh] island. Is it an apology for the cross-examination? I rather think so. Rowed across in the currach by the two Willies. Pleasant walk, but it is a grim place. Not much of interest either. Just the site of a few huts in the S[outh], the slab, and the standing stone surrounded by a circle which they say is the tomb of a dog (...?)

✎ Tuesday, 20 June ✎

Rain all morning. Had dinner early and went to work from 2 to 7, so only 3 of the extra hours used up. Remains 4.

The men rather forlornly digging up white sand E[ast] of [House] 3, not realizing that they are just making breathing space to excavate [House] 5 (at the N[orth] of [House] 3). Shake their heads when I try to explain [...]

---

15 Garda, or guard, is an Irish policeman.

ၹ Wednesday, 21 June ୧

[...]

The men go on clearing in the sheep-pen. Will have to clear stones on top of wall of room tomorrow. The gloom of the men was caused by the fear of having to cart again all the white sand. Obviously they have read the licence which I had left purposely on my table!

I don't intend to fill in with sand, which would be soft, and consequently more dangerous than holes. Anyway the buildings are worth preserving. I shall ask to have them scheduled, and I shall make some stone walls to protect any dangerous hole.

They brightened noticeably when they realized that!

The bones pass without any comment since my conversation with the guard.[16]

1 hour extra. [...]

ၹ Saturday, 24 June ୧

[...]

Back for dinner at 2 o'c[lock]. Rain. The men ask to go at once to Seán Ph[ádin]'s boat, which will take them to the mainland. This means 2 extra hours used up, plus 3 for Tuesday morning. Remains 4 hours.

Paid full week in consequence.

In the evening, met A[nn] wandering about the island with a segment of cork-filling of a lifebuoy. Comment: It will be excellent for the dinner tomorrow! ... (as fuel of course).

Seals everywhere – at the Drack, three of them, full of curiosity, one nearly white. Bathing with delight in the rising tide. Three others in the curved sandy bay N[orth] of the ruined house, another under the Bailey Mór – sign of bad weather – and worse still, one at the Porteen.

ၹ Sunday, 25 June ୧

Wanted to go on the other side of the Drack, but miscalculated the tide.

Wind very strong. The boats don't come back.

Made map of the island and measured roughly position of various groups of ruins.

16 Garda King.

81 Quern stone in excavation area.

❧ Monday, 26 June ❧

Wind calming down. Still no boats. Peaceful morning photographing and drawing querns near St Col[um Cille]'s Ch[urch] and inspecting the Bailey Beg. Come back when one of the sharkers[17] in sight. But goes to the factory ship[18] at the other island, and no currachs seem to appear. Suddenly Ann signals a currach going to the strand under the excavations. I go to meet it. Two fishermen plus Pateen and Little Willie with my post and some messages. We go back to the house where dinner is more or less getting ready. Whilst we are starting, the two others appear, out of another currach. Six hours of work in the afternoon, so two extra hours left.

    [...]

    This evening, went walking on the cliffs, in a cool, lovely wind. The sea in motion by big, heavy waves which come crashing on the rocks. The seagulls quite mad, diving with a swishing noise over my head, and doing the most extraordinary turns by letting themselves be whirled around by the wind. The oyster-catchers equally mad; one of them chasing a seagull; the cheek of it for somebody who makes such a poor show in the air! Found the first mushrooms, shining white in the half dried up grass. The yellow irises are still

17 Sailboats that meet shark vessels.   18 Large ocean ship with fish processing facilities.

in flower here and there, specially along that queer stream which runs towards the edge of the cliff. The other flowers are knotted close to the ground, without a stem: some little pink gentians, a deep red orchid, some *serpolet* [wild thyme], and a little umbel, which opens straight out of its root in the middle of a light crown of leaves [*small sketch of flower*]. A few crows have appeared these last days on the cliffs.

[...]

✢ Wednesday, 28 June ✢

Rotten weather, wind, rain etc. etc. No work in the morning. Dinner early. Started about 1 o'cl[ock]. At 5, rain again, stopped. So 4 hours. They owe me 1 hour.

[...]

Mist. The Mullet, Achill have disappeared. Only the very white foam of the waves rushing at the S[outh] shore very distinct. The sharker at the S[outh] island like the ghost of a boat.

✢ Thursday, 29 June ✢

The men, who had protested with indignation when I suggested not working on Corpus Christi, nearly go on strike today.[19] John Reilly, who passes on his way to the currach, remarks: You will be working on a Sunday next![20] Hadn't seen that I was just behind him. I tell him that I have definite instructions at which he looks a bit sheepish. After dinner, I show the paper from the OPW to the men. They scan it in all directions, including upside down, and approve. Willie Mór, to show how well travelled he is, remarks: sure, in America, they work even on Sundays. Then, after another reading of the paper, he looks at me with horror and exclaims: So, in this kind of work, you have to work on the Bank Holiday? – This, to him, seems much worse than Peter and Paul! [...]

19 29 June is the feast of SS Peter and Paul.   **20** Henry herself nearly always did some excavation work on Sundays, along with house tasks such as painting windows or making curtains. She also continues to dig and draw and conjecture about the finds on the days when the men are not present to help. Sometimes Ann must have helped, as she notes objects that Ann found.

❧ Sunday, 2 July ❧

Gone at last on the other side of the Drak. The cows seldom get there, so lots of flowers. Part of rock garden. Nests of seagulls, but only one with eggs.
[...]
In the afternoon, visit of G[arda] King, very friendly, and very interested.

❧ Monday, 3 July ❧

The men only come back about 12.30. Work from 2 to 7. They owe me 3 hours for that morning and 1 hour from last week = 4 hours.
[...]

❧ Monday, 10 July ❧

The sea pretty rough. A currach appears in the morning. When near, proves to be the two fishermen (John Reilly[21] and Pat Johnny Eamon).[22] We go to meet them at the Porteen. They land with the news that Pateen has removed himself to Achill, and is staying with his married daughter. They[23] have replaced him by a young boy, Seán Monaghan. They have the flour. But the sea is rough for a loaded currach. God knows when they will come!
[...]

❧ Tuesday, 11 July ❧

The sea still high, though the wind has gone down. No currach. Begin to wonder if they will come back at all!
[...]

❧ Wednesday, 12 July ❧

Went down to the B[ailey] M[ór]. After a while, saw the currach coming. The men have tea, then come to work at 12.

---

21 John Terreen Reilly.   22 Pat Johnny Éamon O Muineacháin.   23 Here she is referring to the other workers, who have not yet returned from the mainland.

[...]

Ann brings me tea, and we sit on other side, beside the entrance of the beehive. Suddenly, looking up, I see a face staring – or grinning – at me from the little pillar I have brought yesterday, the sun being right on it. The weirdest effect!

Visit of two men from the sharker.

❧ Friday, 14 July ❧

Labour trouble! Labour trouble, heavens, what trouble!! All about a half bag of potatoes which <u>they</u> say they dug and for which <u>they</u> say I should pay them (three of them!!) a day's work. I could easily dig that much in three hours all by myself, and anyway Ann swears that they belong to a man in Fallmore who dug them himself for Máire Keane, whom I am to pay – as I thought. I will probably never know the truth of the whole thing. Anyway, I saw red, told them that they hadn't done a stroke of work the whole morning, and to stop talking nonsense. As by a miracle, they became lambs, and did work. Willie Beag chose to go to the fair tomorrow in Belmullet, and left at 1 o'c[lock] in John Reilly's currach. So he is supposed to have done 4 hours today, though he did nothing but look at the clouds. So he has 1 day and 6 hours. 1 extra hour to each other man. S[eán] M[onaghan] (who is very good) has three full days, the others 2 days and 3 hours.

[...]

❧ Saturday, 15 July ❧

[...]

In the afternoon, violent gale with furious squalls blowing from the S[outh], and beating, slashing rain. Work in between sheltering under the wall, in spite of a lumbago in my right ribs. Decide to clear grass to the W[est] of house. Suddenly, when hacking at a top sod with the trowel, exactly below the last S[outh] slab, a bronze brooch jumps at me! Cross between pen[annular] br[ooch] and ring pins.[24] Clinches the whole matter of dates. Probably seventh [century].

[...]

24 Ring and straight pin used to fasten clothing.

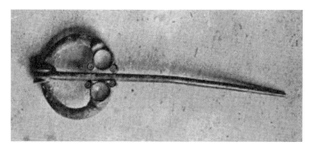

82 One of the bronze pins Françoise Henry found during the excavations at Inishkea North during 1950 (from Françoise Henry, 'A wooden hut on Inishkea North, Co. Mayo', *JRSAI*, 82 (1952), 163–78, pl. XXVII, facing p. 169).

✆ Monday, 17 July[25] ✆

[...]

1 extra hour.

Willie Beag	1 day	6 hours
Seán Monaghan	5 days	1 hours
Willie Mór	4 days	4 hours
Pat Monaghan	4 days	4 hours

✆ Wednesday, 19 July ✆

Willie didn't come back last night. Overheard the men saying that he had probably left with a batch of workmen going to England. Worried a lot during the night; liver probably. The sharkers haven't come back either, and the factory boat is unattended at the S[outh] island. For the first time felt rather cut off. Worried about the pay-sheets which I had had to give to Willie so that Pat's son would sign them.[26]

---

25 The second notebook for 1950 picks up during the archaeological notes for this date. 26 She is employing Pat only by pretending he is his son, as he is legally too old. His son lives on the mainland.

At morning tea, the following conversation goes on: that sharker, there is nobody left on her. – There is coal there ... (We are getting short of turf) – Oh, let's go with the currach! – <u>Me</u>: If you do that, the work will be stopped immediately (visions of the shark-fishing Co., or whatever it is, suing the O[ffice] [of] P[ublic] W[orks] about stolen coal! ...) <u>Ann</u> (meditatively) ... Perhaps it wouldn't be right? ...

About 12 o'cl[ock], the men announce two currachs, though I can't see a thing. Pat and W[illie] Mór comment: people coming for sheep, probably. But Seán Monaghan, authoritatively states: not at all, it's John Reilly and his mate in one currach, and Willie Willie (W[illie] Beag) with Seán Willie,[27] his brother in the other. – How the devil he knew ... but it was true, thank God! Willie, without potatoes, commenting to Ann: I suppose <u>she</u> will murder me! Ann, who comes with a grin to bring the news, adds that his brother is staying until Saturday, and that she has just been making tea for everybody (I am not sure the sheep are not included). Upon which I have an inspiration, and answer: tell Willie that I <u>won't</u> murder him if his brother comes to work with us. Well, half an hour later, I look up from H[ouse] 11 where I am working, and I see above the wall of 7–8 a strange figure in a very tawny brown suit (complete with fountain pen in pocket), gummed hair and sea-boots, wielding a spade with such gusto that I fly at once to the spot to see if there is a wall left intact. But not at all, he had got into the game beautifully, and comments from time to time: I don't see any bones! (What stories has he heard, goodness knows!!) Willie looking extremely sheepish.

All afternoon, the work goes as by magic, and the worst of the sand-cliff has disappeared by evening. If the weather holds, we may finish *complexe* [*sic*] 3 by the end of the week.

[...]

Thursday		
Willie Beag	3 days	
Seán Cawley	1 day	4 h[ours] ½
Seán Monaghan	8 days	3 hours
Willie Mór	7 days	6 hours
Pat Monaghan	7 days	6 hours

Seán and Willie Cawley have done 6 hours each. 1 hour extra to the others.

27 This man is listed on her pay notes, two pages later, as Seán Cawley. Willie Beag is Willie Cawley.

83 'Strange steps in the kitchen'. Cow entering door of 'Sweeney House' on Inishkea North.

❧ Thursday, 20 July ❧

Willie Beag, having drunk too much porter (last night? or on the mainland?), disappears after dinner. Has done 4 hours. His brother disappears also at about 4.30. Removes himself from the island in a currach which comes for sheep. Has done 5½ hours. 1 hour extra to the others.

    [...]

    Said to W[illie] M[ór]: I don't suppose you could put that lintel in position, being only three? W[illie]: sure, Willie will do that for you. – We go and inspect the stone. W[illie]: it's a mighty big stone, we couldn't without Willie Beag. Seán: it's no bigger than the one we have just put up (it was only three-quarters its size). They put it up. Willie (looking at me with triumph): Well, now, aren't we strong!

    Went to the Drack tonight. The sea very strong, glassy blue, touched with a pink light. Six seals at the Drack. Four of them enormous, heaving their triangular heads out of the water to stare at me. The cattle on this island is [*sic*] too tame. The other day I was alone in the house, Ann having gone for water to the well. Noise of violent cavalcade outside. Strange steps in the kitchen. I open the door and find the black and white calf – the one I call White Socks – sheltering behind the table from its enemy the red calf. Stared at me with its big liquid eyes. Did not like at all the remark that I didn't approve of calves inside the house. Got him out, and had to pet it for at least ten minutes to calm it from its fright. Wherever I meet it, it just lifts its head and waits for me to pat the white patch on its forehead. The others have a slightly more coy way of greeting you, but most of them end by thrusting their heads at your hand.

Index